125 True Stories of Amazing Pets

INSPIRING TALES OF ANIMAL FRIENDSHIP & FOUR-LEGGED HEROES, PLUS CRAZY ANIMAL ANTICS

Zorro the pig catches some waves. Check him out on page 17!

NATIONAL GEOGRAPHIC KiDS

WASHINGTON, D.C.

Contents

Introduction 6
Skateboarding Mouse 8
Tubby the Labrador
 Protects the Planet 10
Darius the Giant Rabbit 11
Dog Stranded on Ice 11
Elderly Zoo Gorilla
 Has Pet Bunny 12
Pet Giraffe 13
Justin the Horse
 Loves to Paint 13
Goat Rides Donkey 14
Dog Fetches Tissues
 When Owner Sneezes 15
Cheesecake the Capybara . . . 15
Blind Pup Has Guide Dog 16
Jumping Gerbil 17
Surfing Pig Catches Waves . . . 17
Got Air? 18
6 Pampered Pets 20
Rupert the Giant Cat 26
Pepper the Rat 27
Rowdy the Rat Terrier
 Saves Neighbor 27
Tater Tot the Helper Horse . . 28
Grumpy Cat 29
Diamond the Pit Bull Saves
 Family From Fire 29

Spaniel Has Pet Owl 30
Parrot Pedals Bike 32
Cat Guides Blind Dog 33
Chicken Walks on Leash 33
Pig in Boots! 34
Cat Has 26 Toes! 35
Donkey Saves Sheep 35
Seeing-Eye Horse 36
Cat Flashes Golden Smile . . . 37
Dog Swallows 111 Pennies . . . 37
Cat Runs for Mayor 38
Dog Walks on "Hands" 39
Horse Works Magic 39
Cat Gets Swimming Lessons . . 40
Half Zebra, Half Donkey 41

Pooch Paints Pictures 41
Stoosh the Pet Skunk 42
Soccer Collie Scores Goals . . . 43
World's Oldest Pig 43
8 Real Animal Heroes! 44
Naughty Dog Buys Stuff 50
Florida the Turtle 51
Microchip Locates Lost Cat . . 51
Jack of All Trades 52
Dog Bottle-Feeds Sheep 54
Hamster Robot Pilot 55
Panda Cow 55
Pig Has Wheels for Legs 56
Dog Runs on Cross-
 Country Team 57

Dogs Drive Car
Page 58

Horse Plays B-Ball
Page 85

Parrot Saves Toddler...... 57
Dogs Drive Car......... 58
Double-Dutch Dog....... 60
Cat Runs for Senate...... 61
Kid Power............. 61
Cats Become Models!..... 62
Three-Legged
  Jumping Goat......... 63
Dog Runs Road Race..... 63
Dog Scooters Kitty....... 64
Rat Birthday Party....... 65
Parrot Clucks Like Chicken... 65
Ducks March On!........ 66
Flying Guinea Pig........ 67
Tortoise Takes Long Walks... 67
Bunny Hop!............ 68
One Fine Ferret......... 69
Dog Becomes Archaeologist.. 69
Sheep Takes Walks With Dogs. 70
Pup Scout............. 71
Rooster Struts in Boots.... 71
Shadow the Dog Soars..... 72
Otter Loves Dogs........ 74
Owl Rides Dog......... 75
Fluffy Bull............ 75
Dog Wears Wigs........ 76

Dog Mothers Tiger Cubs.... 78
Famous Goat........... 79
Cockatoo Makes Tools..... 79
6 Silly Pet Tricks......... 80
World's Tallest Horse...... 86
Lizard Lives Large....... 87
Pooch Saves Family...... 87
Duck Fashion Show....... 88
Dog Flies Away......... 89
Cat Rescues Owner....... 89
Dog Rides Scooter....... 90
Cat Takes Trip......... 91
Donkey Heroes......... 91
Cat Has Two Faces...... 92
Chihuahua Chases
  Away Burglars........ 93
Cockatoo Beats the Odds... 93
Camel Dines With Owners... 94
Dog Protects Piglet...... 95

Cat Gets Bionic Feet...... 95
Puppy Saves Friend
  From Bees........... 96
Alpaca Rides the Waves.... 97
Kitty Crime Spree....... 97
Monkey Helps Out....... 98
Four-Eared Cat......... 98
Puppy-Sitting Hen!...... 99
Cow Jumps Hurdles..... 100
Kai the Wolf-Pup Nanny... 101
Spoiled Swine......... 101
Horses Roam
  the House.......... 102
Furriest Feline........ 104
Rabbit Thinks She's
  a Leopard.......... 105
Cat Waits for Train...... 105
Going Out With a Splash!.. 106
Index.............. 108
Credits............. 111

Introduction

WELCOME to the zany, hilarious, and heartwarming world of amazing pets!

Paw through these pages and find 125 of National Geographic Kids' favorite true tales of animal heroes, silly tricks, spoiled-rotten critters, and even pets that have pets of their own. Meet Mog, the cat that isn't afraid of water. Check out Cali, the miniature horse that helps her blind owner get to school. And be a guest at a fashion show where you'll see some FABulous geese.

These weird-but-true stories are not only fun to read, but they may also push the limits of what humans think our pets can do. So prepare to be amazed by these furry, feathered, and finned friends who are just a little bit different from your average pet!

Norman the dog has ridden a scooter since he was a puppy. Check him out on page 90!

This pet mouse has a knack for skateboarding.

TUBBY THE LABRADOR

PROTECTS THE PLANET

TORFAEN, WALES, U.K.
Everyone knows it's cool to recycle, but would you expect a dog to be into it? Over the past eight years, ten-year-old Tubby the yellow Labrador retriever has collected more than 30,000 plastic bottles for his owner to recycle. On his daily walks, he digs bottles out from under bushes and wades into creeks to fetch them.

"I think he likes the noise he makes when he crushes them," says Tubby's owner, Sandra Gilmore. "Once he went through the snow up the mountain and found a big plastic bottle. Then he carried it all the way home."

This doggy recycling unit even takes the tops off before giving plastic bottles to his owner. Why? This pooch may be yellow, but he's the greenest dog around.

Labrador retrievers are the most popular breed of dog in the U.S.

WHAT'S UP, DOC?

DARIUS THE GIANT RABBIT

WORCESTER, ENGLAND, U.K.
Darius is no ordinary bunny—from ear tip to tail he's four feet four inches (1.3 m) long. That's about as long as the average ten-year-old kid is tall! This furry 50-pound (22.7 kg) creature is a Flemish giant rabbit, a breed known for its size. He loves to lounge around the house eating snacks while watching his favorite shows on TV.

What does a giant rabbit eat? In addition to his meals, which consist of rabbit chow, apples, and cabbage, Darius snacks on—what else?—carrots *with* their leafy tops, please. Up to 12 a day.

The Flemish giant rabbit is sometimes called the "gentle giant" because of its easy-going nature.

DOG STRANDED ON ICE

WOOF?

Baltic kept slipping and falling into the icy water as the ship's crew tried to pull him up.

GDYNIA, POLAND
Baltic the dog is an official crew member of a research ship. His life is pretty cushy now—he even gets his own stylish life vest—but it hasn't always been that way. He survived an icy ordeal and was rescued by the ship before he got the job. For two days and nights Baltic clung to a chunk of ice drifting down the Vistula River in Poland. No one knows how the dog ended up stranded on the ice floe that he rode like a frozen raft for 85 miles (137 km), or how he survived the frigid, watery adventure. Eventually he ended up in the icy Baltic Sea, surrounded by seals that wanted to make a meal out of him.

An engineer aboard the ship used an inflatable raft to rescue Baltic. Adam Buczynski wrapped him in blankets and snuggled up with him that night to keep him warm. To everyone's amazement, the dog had no injuries or ailments from his ordeal. "Ever since the moment I took him into my hands," says Buczynski, "Baltic sticks close to me. And everybody loves him very much."

ELDERLY ZOO GORILLA HAS PET BUNNY

IS IT TIME FOR MY HOPPING LESSON?

ERIE, PENNSYLVANIA, U.S.A.
Samantha the western lowland gorilla seemed to like her new roommate, Panda the Dutch rabbit. But her keepers at the Erie Zoo grew worried one day when the rabbit hopped over to Samantha's favorite stuffed animal. They knew the ape was crazy about her toy and feared 200-pound (91 kg) Samantha might get upset if the rabbit got too close. But the gorilla didn't sweat it. She just moved the toy so Panda could pass by. That's when keepers realized the two roomies were best buds.

Too shy to live with other apes, Samantha was paired with the rabbit to keep from getting lonely. Keepers introduced them slowly, first letting the duo see each other through a mesh screen. Eventually, Panda moved into the ape's exhibit. "Almost immediately, they were sitting side by side," zoo CEO Scott Mitchell says.

The pair were practically inseparable. Together, they liked watching visitors walk by their exhibit, and Samantha often let the rabbit nibble on her hay. Keepers even saw the gorilla stroke Panda under his chin. Says Mitchell, "Their friendship was one of a kind."

PET GIRAFFE

CULLINAN, SOUTH AFRICA
No matter how tall she got, Fenne the orphan giraffe always loved to come inside the house, even when getting through the door became a tight squeeze. As a baby, Fenne would race her human "brothers" around the safari lodge where they lived. "At first it was easy for us to keep up with her," says Craig MacRae, who was a teenager when he found the newborn giraffe near death in the African bush and rescued her. "But as she grew bigger and stronger she would outrun us with ease." When she was five feet (1.5 m) tall, the giraffe followed her owner everywhere he went, leaning on him if he stood still. "My brother and I loved playing pranks on my mom," owner MacRae recalls. "We would sneak Fenne into my parents' bedroom, then wait for my mom's screams about giraffe poop on her carpet."

Fenne the giraffe loved to wear hats and scarves.

JUSTIN THE HORSE LOVES TO PAINT

COLUMBUS, INDIANA, U.S.A.
The day Justin the Artistic Horse picked up a whip with his teeth and made designs in the sand, a lightbulb went off in his owner's head. "He's a smart horse," Adonna Combs says. "I thought, maybe he's telling me he wants to paint."

She grabbed paintbrushes, an easel, and some nontoxic acrylic paint. "He understood right away that the brush was supposed to touch the paper," says Combs, an artist herself. "It was instinct. The more he paints, the better he gets." Justin holds the brush between his teeth and strokes the brush back and forth, or makes circles and zigzags, in a colorful palette. Sometimes he blends the colors (his favorites are blue and green) on the canvas with his strong, wiggly lips. He even paints abstract horselike shapes, including a self-portrait. When he's done, he throws the brush down and "signs" the painting with his hoofprint.

Some of Justin's paintings have sold for as much as $2,500.

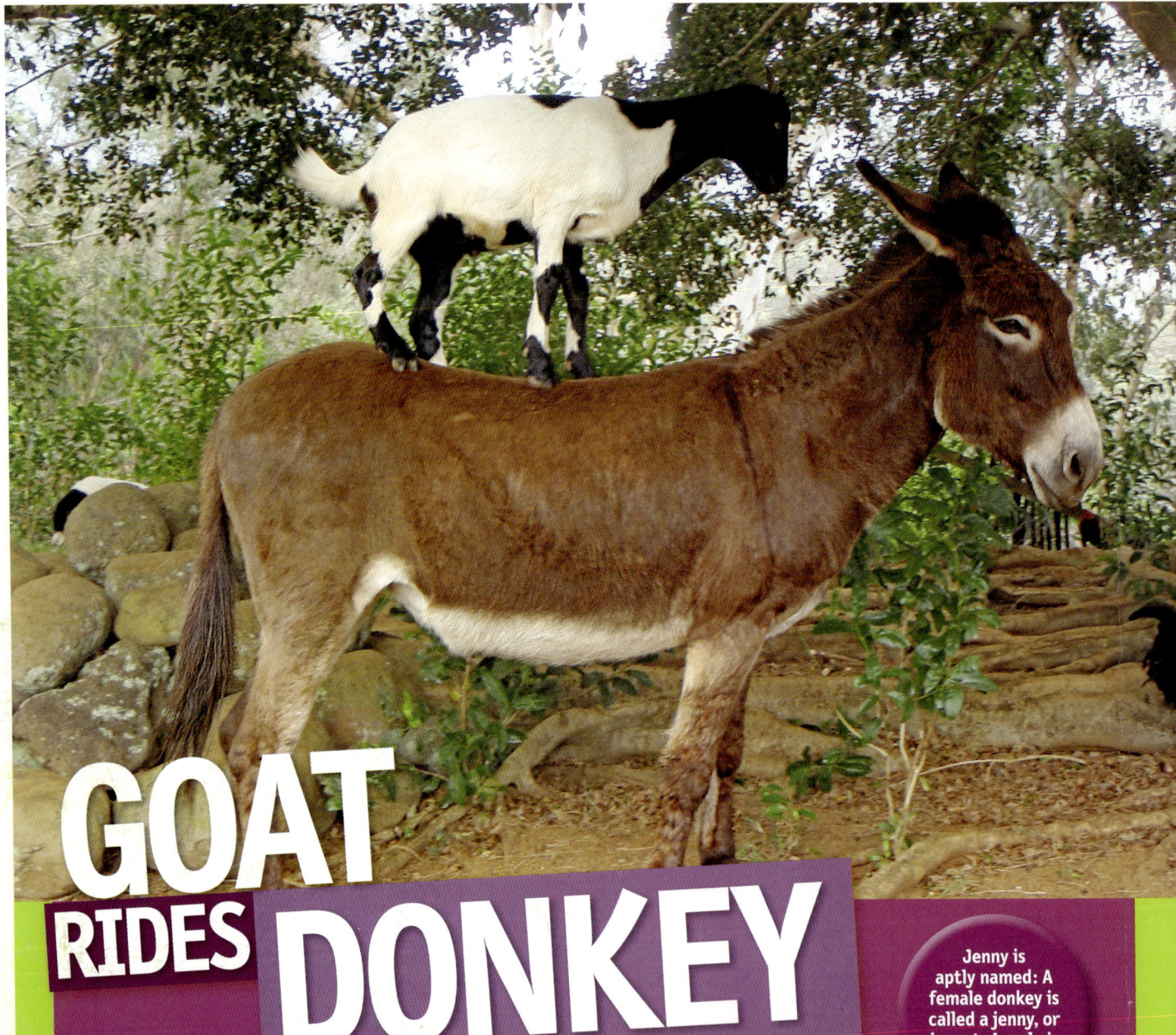

GOAT RIDES DONKEY

Jenny is aptly named: A female donkey is called a jenny, or jennet. A male is called a jack.

HAIKU, HAWAII, U.S.A.
Jenny the donkey carries a kid named Danny on her back. The "kid" is a goat. When they lived together, Jenny let the goat hop up on her back several times a day for free rides around the farm.

"When Danny was little, he loved to jump up onto high places," says Jenny's caregiver Laurelee Blanchard. "Being four and a half feet [1.4 m] up on her back must have made him feel like a king."

Blanchard runs the Leilani Farm Sanctuary, where Jenny is a pampered pet that loves to be brushed.

"Sometimes Danny would lose his balance and fall," Blanchard says. But Jenny always waited for him to jump back on board her wide, furry back. "It must have felt like she was getting a massage," Blanchard adds. "Jenny's sweet and gentle. She carries the goat around for sheer enjoyment." No kidding!

DOG FETCHES TISSUES WHEN OWNER SNEEZES

Terrier breeds range in size from just a couple of pounds to over 70 pounds (1–32 kg).

DOBBS FERRY, NEW YORK, U.S.A.
"Achoo!" When Harper the terrier mix hears her best friend sneeze, the dog perks her ears, dashes to retrieve a tissue, and delivers it to the girl. A few years ago, Molly Winiarski and her family adopted Harper and promised to give the four-pound (1.8 kg) pup a great life.

From the start, Harper had loads of energy. "When we first came home," says Molly, "my mom fell asleep on the porch swing with little Harper. The pup chewed the rope that holds the swing and it fell. That's when I knew she was going to be trouble."

Molly got busy coaching the puppy to "burn energy and train her brain," she says. Now the dog knows more than 70 tricks, like jumping rope, skateboarding, and ringing a bell. But what if Harper doesn't feel like training? "Then I start working with our other dog, Willow, and tell her how good she is," Molly says. "Then Harper flies out to show that she can do it better."

CHEESECAKE THE CAPYBARA

MIDWAY, ARKANSAS, U.S.A.
Like a mother duck leading her babies, Cheesecake the capybara is at the head of a parade. But her followers aren't ducklings, or even baby capybaras. They're abandoned dachshund puppies. The seven pups love to wrestle with their 55-pound (25 kg) rodent babysitter. When they tire of playing, the dachshunds march into Cheesecake's heated pen and curl up next to the capybara in a supersize puppy pile.

The day the orphaned dachshunds arrived, Rocky Ridge Refuge owner Janice Wolf didn't have much time to prepare. Cheesecake's pen was the only place available to keep the tiny pups away from the other rescued animals, such as dogs, tortoises, deer, birds, rabbits, and even a miniature horse. "Cheesecake was thrilled to have the puppies," Wolf says. But if the pups are naughty—like when they try to grab hay out of the capybara's mouth—Cheesecake isn't afraid to discipline them. "She makes a cute little squeaky noise to scold them," Wolf says.

The dachshunds have since been adopted, but a new litter of orphaned pit bull pups has arrived. "I keep an eye on them," Wolf says. "But Cheesecake does all the work. She's the best nanny ever."

BLIND PUP HAS GUIDE DOG

Eddy (left) wears a plastic mask to protect his face.

CARDIFF, WALES, U.K.

Eddy the Labrador retriever loves splashing in a creek near his home. But often the blind dog is unable to find his way back to the bank. That's when Milo the mixed terrier steps in, barking so Eddy can follow his voice to the creek's edge. The "guide dog" then grabs on to the Lab's protective face shield to lead him to dry land.

Eddy and Milo have been best buds for years. When Eddy lost his sight, Milo acted as the pooch's very own guide. Indoors, Eddy follows Milo's scent, which helps Eddy avoid bumping into furniture. If the blind pooch wanders away outside, Milo runs off to find him and lead him home. The terrier even sits protectively on Eddy's back while the Lab sleeps.

"Eddy and Milo have a strong bond," dog behaviorist Mary Burch says. "Milo cares for Eddy, and Eddy pays more attention to sounds and smells so he can follow Milo." The pair uses teamwork even at play. "They love running around together holding the ends of a giant branch in their mouths," owner Angie Baker-Stedham says. "Eddy would be lost without Milo."

Labrador retrievers can be one of three colors: yellow, chocolate, or black.

JUMPING GERBIL

WALTHAM, MASSACHUSETTS, U.S.A.
On your mark, get set, GERBIL! Diamond leaps over a hurdle and scoots under a fence. He loves running the obstacle course that owner Donna Anastasi has designed, and he gets faster each time he does it. Diamond can master a course quickly, but then he gets bored. Sometimes he just stops and lies down during a run. Then Anastasi knows it's time to change the course to something new.

More and more owners are doing "agility" training with their gerbils. "This is naturally what gerbils like to do," Anastasi says. "They like to run and to go over and under things." Many trainers use food as a treat when a gerbil has mastered a new skill. Anastasi uses a play box—a fun space where Diamond can play after working on the obstacle course. "You can train gerbils to learn new skills very quickly," Anastasi concludes. "You can teach an entire course in just a couple of hours!"

The average adult gerbil weighs about two and a half ounces (71 g), about as much as a tennis ball.

SURFING PIG CATCHES WAVES

MY LIFE IS ANYTHING BUT A BOAR!

MOUNT MAUNGANUI, NEW ZEALAND
When Matthew Bell catches a gnarly wave, his best buddy, Zorro, goes along for the ride, balancing nimbly on the surfboard. "I always thought it would be a fun idea to surf with a pig," Bell says. "So one day I did." Zorro loves the beach and is always ready to go out into the water. What happens when the two surfers wipe out in a big wave? Zorro simply "pig paddles" back to shore. "Pigs are phenomenal swimmers," Bell says.

Zorro grunts his excitement whenever it's time to climb aboard the surfboard. Says Bell, "If you could ask Zorro what his three favorite things are, he would answer 1) surfing, 2) eating, and 3) surfing."

Zorro is part kunekune pig, a small breed native to New Zealand.

GOT AIR?

I BETTER GET A TREAT FOR THIS!

Former U.S. President Bill Clinton owned a chocolate Lab named Buddy when he was in office.

RIVERSIDE, IOWA, U.S.A.

Jordan the chocolate Labrador retriever is a canine torpedo and a champion dock diver. She once broke a world record by launching 31 feet 2 inches (9.5 m)—that's as long as a stretch limo!—off a dock into a pool. What a splash!

Jordan and her owner, Sean McCarthy, have traveled to 22 states in the U.S. for competitions. To stay in shape for her dives, Jordan runs daily on a treadmill and gets a massage before and after competitions.

Jordan loved water from the very first time she cannonballed into a pond at the dog park. Every time they returned to the park, McCarthy noticed that Jordan would jump off the bank instead of running straight into the water like other dogs. McCarthy trained her to jump farther and farther by throwing balls and Frisbees into the water. "She would jump into a pool of fire to get the toy," says McCarthy, who named his dog after his childhood hero, the basketball star Michael Jordan.

"As it turns out," he says, "she became an 'Air Jordan' all on her own."

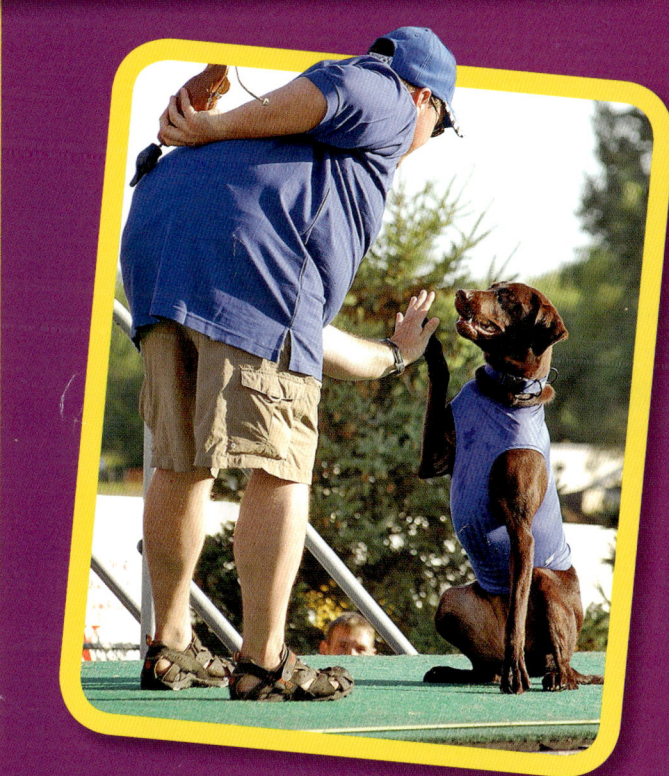

6 PAMPERED PETS

Some pet owners like to shower their animals with love and treats. These stories are all about spoiled-rotten pets that get around in style!

1 PRESIDENTIAL POOCH

WASHINGTON, D.C., U.S.A.
When things didn't work out with his first owners, Bo was returned to the breeder. His next home? The White House! The Obamas received Bo as a gift from Senator Ted Kennedy in April 2009. Since then, the Portuguese water dog has become a beloved member of the First Family. Because of allergies, Malia Obama needed a dog that wouldn't shed its hair, and Bo fit the bill perfectly. Known as the First Dog of the United States, he romps with Malia and Sasha on the White House lawn. Bo even has access to the Oval Office, where President Obama works. According to the White House, Bo's favorite food is "tomatoes—or toys." Bo is one lucky dog!

U.S. President Woodrow Wilson kept a herd of sheep on the White House lawn.

NOW THIS IS A TURTLENECK!

The average Russian tortoise is eight to nine inches (20–23 cm) long, as long as an unsharpened pencil.

2 COZY TORTOISE

VANCOUVER, WASHINGTON, U.S.A.
Is that a little stegosaurus bumbling through the yard? Nope. It's Roz the pint-size Russian tortoise sporting a crocheted "cozy" made by his owner, artist Katie Bradley. "The first time I put the stegosaurus cozies on the tortoises, it looked so funny and prehistoric when they walked all about. My two-year-old said, 'Me have dinosaurs now!'"

Bradley originally made a variety of cozies—flowers, vegetables, and animals—for her seven pet tortoises as a joke, then realized they were handy for spotting them in the grass when she let them out to roam in the garden. "As tortoises are cold-blooded, a cozy doesn't actually keep them warm," Bradley says. "But seeing a little pumpkin zooming about in the tall grass is pretty hilarious."

With help from Roz as a model, Bradley sells her tortoise cozies to customers all over the world. "Roz is very patient about being photographed," Bradley says. "One time he made a very handsome shark." Roz's favorite outfit? A perfectly delicious cheeseburger!

3 FASHIONISTA GUINEA PIG

TOKYO, JAPAN
Latte the guinea pig is ready for his glamour shot. He's the star of a photo shoot for fashion designer Maki Yamada's line of clothing. She calls it Guinea Pig Fashion. Latte models tiaras, tank tops, hats, Santa costumes, traditional Japanese kimonos, wigs, wedding dresses, and even ninja costumes.

But the life of a fashion model can be exhausting. "One time he was so happy, running and hopping around the kitchen, before I could undress him," Yamada says, "and he fell asleep still wearing his wardrobe."

The pros outweigh the cons, however. Latte is highly paid with mounds of fresh, crunchy veggies.

The guinea pig is native to South America and was first domesticated around 5000 B.C.

THEY SAY I'M RAM-BUNCTIOUS.

4 PIERCE THE SHEEP

WOODLAND HILLS, CALIFORNIA, U.S.A.
Sit, stay, and roll over are normal tricks for a dog, but what about for a sheep? Trained by Alice Christensen, a veterinary technology student, Pierce the sheep does many of the same tricks dogs do. The crowd laughs and hoots when he performs at animal shows, where he steals the spotlight from the dogs doing the same tricks! Pierce learned one trick at a time over several months and now can follow more than 16 different commands. "Pierce loves to learn," Christensen says. "He brightens up the whole college campus when they see him do tricks. He's the school mascot!"

There are approximately one billion sheep in the world.

Pierce the sheep runs through a Hula-Hoop at an animal show.

5 HORSE FLIES FIRST CLASS

WELLINGTON, FLORIDA, U.S.A.
"Another mint, please!" That's what Cedric the Olympic show-jumping horse might ask his flight attendant—if he could talk, that is. For the past nine years, the VIP frequent flier has circled the globe, jetting to horse shows in style, crunching his favorite mints along the way. When it's time to hop on a flight, the horse doesn't wait in line, check his bags, or squeeze into an economy-size seat. Instead, he clip-clops into a comfy, custom-made box stall. In-flight service includes an all-you-can-eat hay buffet and gallons of fresh water. But this equine traveler doesn't horse around during his flights. "Cedric likes to relax when he's flying and eats the entire time," says his travel agent, concierge, and manager, Mary Elizabeth Kent. He also travels with his Olympic rider, his groom, his vet, and his favorite friends—a team of massage therapists!

Many U.S. commercial airlines allow domesticated cats, small dogs, rabbits, and birds to fly in the cabin with their owners, in carriers of course!

Over 56 million households in the U.S. own dogs, while over 45 million households own cats.

6 LION POODLE

MOORE, OKLAHOMA, U.S.A.
Falcor the poodle is ready to roar! His "lion look" is so realistic that people are often frightened when he walks by. Professional dog groomer Lori Craig has been entering Falcor in dog-grooming competitions since 2004, often winning. Craig loves creating animal hairstyles. Over the years, Falcor has been a panda, a clownfish, and a baboon. "The longest part of the process is growing out the hair," Craig says. To create the lion character, Falcor's hair had to grow for four years before it could be dyed. It took more than 40 hours of grooming to make him king of the jungle, she says. That may be a lot of work, but when Halloween comes around, Falcor definitely won't need to shop for a costume!

PUT ME DOWN RIGHT MEOW!

RUPERT THE GIANT CAT

Rupert, a Maine coon cat, has extra-large paws that act like snowshoes.

YARRA GLEN, VICTORIA, AUSTRALIA

Rupert is a GIANT superstar in Australia. He's a celebrated show cat and—at about 20 pounds (9 kg)—he is one of the biggest cats around. But he's no fat cat. "Rupert is lean and muscular just as a show cat should be," says his owner, Kyra Foster.

At home, Rupert leads a typical cat life: eat, sleep, chase a few things, sleep, sleep, sleep. But at cat shows, regal Rupert is the cat's meow. He struts his stuff and poses for the cameras.

"By the end of a show day," Foster says, "he gets a bit sick of it all, turns his back to everyone, and goes to sleep." Good luck trying to move him!

PEPPER THE RAT

PHILADELPHIA, PENNSYLVANIA, U.S.A.

Pepper the rat can do almost anything. He fetches objects on command, jumps hurdles, and opens cupboards. He even puts tiny toy socks into a cardboard washing machine for playtime. This talented rat earned an invitation to appear on the TV show *America's Got Talent*, but owner Abby Roeser declined. She told the show's producers that her rat performs well only in the privacy of her home.

Roeser says Pepper learns quickly and seems to enjoy doing the tricks. "The most rewarding thing is teaching him tricks people have never seen rats do before." Who knows what Pepper will learn next?

About half a million U.S. households own pet rats or mice.

ROWDY THE RAT TERRIER SAVES NEIGHBOR

RANCHO CORDOVA, CALIFORNIA, U.S.A.

Rowdy the rat terrier went barking mad when he walked by the storm drain where a dog named Casper was trapped. Rowdy barked and barked, trying to tell his owner that he had sniffed out the 15-year-old dog that had been missing from their neighborhood for three days. Casper was stuck deep down an eight-inch (20 cm) pipe below the street.

When Rowdy's owner realized that Rowdy had found Casper, she ran to her neighbor's house for help. Soon firefighters arrived and rescued the scared, wet dog from the pipe.

Ready Rowdy may not have known it, but he's always been a natural-born animal tracker. Rat terriers were bred to hunt animals below the ground. Good dog, Rowdy!

Rat terriers are a long-living dog breed. They often live to be 12 to 18 years old.

TATER TOT
THE HELPER HORSE

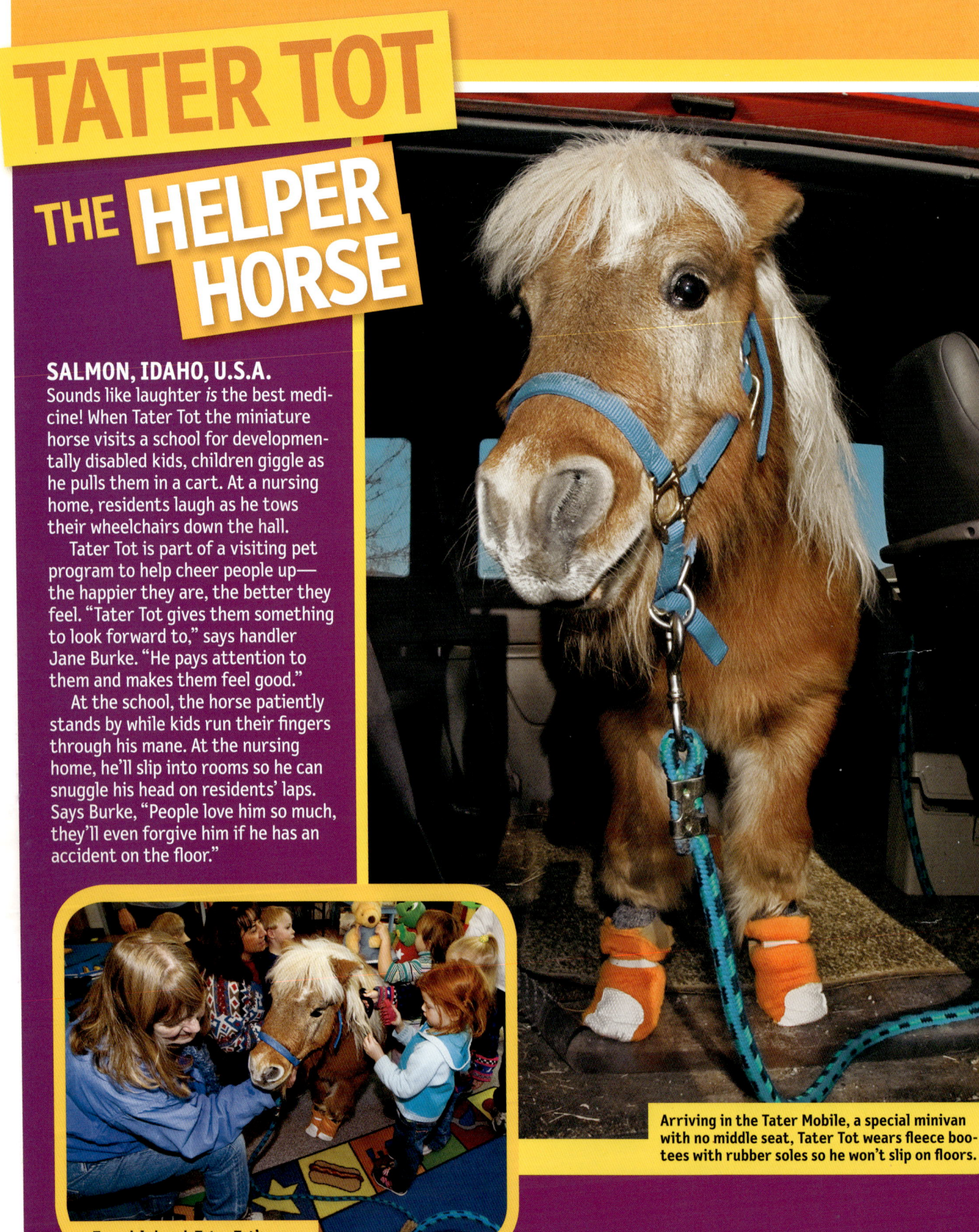

Arriving in the Tater Mobile, a special minivan with no middle seat, Tater Tot wears fleece bootees with rubber soles so he won't slip on floors.

SALMON, IDAHO, U.S.A.
Sounds like laughter *is* the best medicine! When Tater Tot the miniature horse visits a school for developmentally disabled kids, children giggle as he pulls them in a cart. At a nursing home, residents laugh as he tows their wheelchairs down the hall.

Tater Tot is part of a visiting pet program to help cheer people up—the happier they are, the better they feel. "Tater Tot gives them something to look forward to," says handler Jane Burke. "He pays attention to them and makes them feel good."

At the school, the horse patiently stands by while kids run their fingers through his mane. At the nursing home, he'll slip into rooms so he can snuggle his head on residents' laps. Says Burke, "People love him so much, they'll even forgive him if he has an accident on the floor."

Two girls brush Tater Tot's mane.

GRUMPY CAT

GALION, OHIO, U.S.A.
A frowny feline named Tardar Sauce has made a career out of turning other people's frowns upside down. "Everyone's got something that makes them a little grumpy," her owner, Bryan Bundesen, says. "Her grumpy mug makes people smile."

It all started when Bundesen posted a picture of the cat's pouty face online. Immediately, fans began adding captions to the photo, with the first and most popular being "I had fun once. It was awful." The picture went viral, making Tardar Sauce an Internet "it" girl overnight. "Grumpy Cat" now has her own website, more than a million "likes" on her Facebook page, T-shirts and holiday cards with her face on them, and a movie deal in the works.

But the cat's out of the bag—Grumpy Cat is no sourpuss. "She's lovable and affectionate and loves to curl up on my lap or have her chin scratched," Bundesen says. According to her veterinarian, this two-year-old kitty's famous scowl is likely due to a condition called feline dwarfism. But otherwise she's healthy and happy.

What does *she* think about her fame? "She is oblivious," Bundesen says. "She's slept through most of her TV interviews and appearances." Cat got your tongue, Tardar Sauce?

Tardar Sauce has a brother, named Pokey, that really does have a grumpy personality!

DIAMOND THE PIT BULL SAVES FAMILY FROM FIRE

SALINAS, CALIFORNIA, U.S.A.
"I had never heard Diamond bark before," says her owner, Darryl Steen. With one loud *woof!* 15-month-old Diamond sounded the alarm to Steen and his daughters, Darahne and Sierra (then 9 and 16), who were all sound asleep.

Steen heard her bark and realized the apartment was on fire. He yelled to his daughters. Darahne came running. In the nick of time, Steen lifted her out a window to safety.

"I thought Sierra had passed away," Steen says. Firefighters searched for the girl. They found the dog lying on the mattress that Sierra had hidden under before she passed out.

"The firefighters were amazed that Diamond would stay with my daughter instead of running from the fire," Steen says. "If we didn't have Diamond, there's no way we would be alive today." The brave pooch received a National Hero Dog Award for her lifesaving efforts, along with a year's supply of tasty kibble.

The pit bull's official name is the American Staffordshire terrier, according to the American Kennel Club.

SHE LOOKS TOUGH, BUT SHE'S A HOOT!

The English springer spaniel is known for its outgoing, affectionate nature.

CORNWALL, ENGLAND, U.K.

Before Bramble the owl takes to the sky for her daily flight, Sophi the English springer spaniel clears her for takeoff by licking the bird's beak. "Since the owl was a baby, Sophi has cleaned Bramble's beak," says Sharon Bindon, the dog's owner, who also runs a sanctuary for birds of prey. "Bramble returns the favor and 'beaks' the dog, as if she were grooming Sophi."

The Eurasian eagle owl and spaniel became best friends when two-week-old Bramble arrived at Ancient Art Falconry. "Sophi sniffed and licked the chick," Bindon says. "Soon Bramble hopped down, toddled over to Sophi, and started following her everywhere."

Years later, they're still practically inseparable, even though in the wild this friendship would never exist. A wild owl would prey on small mammals such as mice, rabbits, and even foxes, which are about Sophi's size. "Sophi won't go near most of our birds of prey," Bindon says. But who needs other friends when you've got one that will snuggle down and nap with you in front of the television?

The Eurasian eagle owl has a wingspan that ranges from five to six and a half feet (1.5–2 m).

PARROT PEDALS BIKE

Harlequin macaws can live for more than 50 years.

SAN JOSE, CALIFORNIA, U.S.A.
Polly want a cracker? Pet show audiences cheer as Zachary the 25-year-old harlequin macaw pedals a pint-size bicycle across the stage. He also rides a scooter, opens soda cans, walks a tightrope, and more. He even holds the Guinness World Record for most basketballs slam-dunked by a parrot in a minute. The first trick, the amazing bike-riding stunt, was the hardest to learn, say Zachary's trainers, Ed and Julie Cardoza. It took him six months to master it. Although now officially retired, Zachary "still enjoys doing his tricks for family and friends, or just because," Julie says. Perhaps he'll come out of retirement for—a cracker?

CAT GUIDES BLIND DOG

HE HELPS ME WHEN THINGS GET RUFF!

LLANGAFFO, NORTH WALES, U.K.
Terfel the Labrador retriever lost his sight to cataracts and could no longer walk around the house without bumping into things. He spent most of his time in his basket, according to owner Judy Godfrey-Brown. Then help came in a most unexpected form—a stray cat that arrived at Godfrey-Brown's door one night looking for a home. Once inside, the cat went up to Terfel to make friends and used her paws to gently guide him around the house and garden. She was a natural! Godfrey-Brown named her Pwditat (pwoo-dee-tat), and she's been best buddies with Terfel ever since. Who says cats and dogs can't be friends?

Cataracts, which cause a blurry film (or clouding) over the lens of the eye, are one of the most common eye problems in dogs.

CHICKEN WALKS ON LEASH

NOW I GET WHY THE CHICKEN CROSSED THE ROAD.

Goldie's hen friend Brenda strolls down a city street.

SYDNEY, AUSTRALIA
Goldie the chicken has an *egg*-cellent exercise routine. The big-city bird takes walks wearing a leash. "She loves to explore the street," says owner John Huntington, whose company, City Chicks, teaches city dwellers to care for hens in their yards.

Raising urban chickens like Goldie has become the latest trend in some cities. One reason is because people like the birds' fresh eggs. "But chickens also make great companions," says Ingrid Dimock, also of City Chicks. Some owners become so attached to their feathered friends that they treat the hens the same as dogs—including taking them on daily strolls.

Before Goldie goes on walks, her owner places her in a comfy harness, which attaches to her leash. Unbothered by car noises, the bird moves at a leisurely pace. And she spends as much time pecking around for grub as she does walking. "She's kind of a slowpoke," Huntington says. "But she has a lot of fun."

Not all cities allow people to keep chickens. Check your local laws before getting a pet hen.

These boots were made for walkin'.

PIG IN BOOTS!

THIRSK, ENGLAND, U.K.

Most pigs love wallowing in the mud. Not Cinders. As a piglet, she refused to walk in mud, sometimes even shaking with fear if she couldn't find a way around a puddle. The solution? Boots!

Owner Andrew Keeble found that doll-size boots were a perfect fit for Cinders. Each day, she'd run to have them put on, then trot happily through the mud. The boots solved the problem but didn't explain her strange actions. Veterinarian Bruce Lawhorn of Texas A&M University thinks it might have been a behavioral response. "If Cinders [once] had sore hoof pads while walking in mud, she might have associated the pain with the mud," he says.

Cinders has outgrown her boots and now braves the mud barehoofed. But she still doesn't roll around in it. Getting dirty just isn't this pig's idea of a good time.

A pig's funny-looking snout helps the animal dig.

TALK TO THE PAW.

CAT HAS 26 TOES!

MILWAUKEE, WISCONSIN, U.S.A.
Daniel the cat's paws might make people, well, pause. Most cats have 18 toes, but this tabby was born with 26—an extra two on each foot.

Daniel's additional digits don't stand in his way. "He behaves just like other cats," says Amy Rowell of the Milwaukee Animal Rescue Center, where Daniel lives. His supersize feet sometimes even give him an upper hand. "He's a pro at grasping toys we wave in front of him," Rowell says.

The feline's paws also helped his rescue center. Just before Daniel arrived, the center found out it was going to lose its housing. After people heard about Daniel, many gave the center $26—one dollar for each of Daniel's toes. Soon the center had enough cash to buy a new home. "We may have rescued Daniel," Rowell says, "but then he turned around and saved us."

THANKS FOR SAVING MY WOOL!

DONKEY SAVES SHEEP

SCARBOROUGH, ENGLAND, U.K.
Stanley the sheep was quietly munching on grass near his barn when a runaway dog lunged at him, sinking its teeth into Stanley's side. Terrified, the sheep let out a loud bleat, but the dog refused to unclamp its jaws.

That's when Dotty the donkey sprang into action. She charged at the dog, bit its back, and pinned it to the ground. Finally the dog released its grip on Stanley and ran off. The sheep quickly recovered from the dog bite, and his good pal Dotty became a local hero.

"Donkeys are protective by nature," says veterinarian Elaine Pendlebury, who presented Dotty with an award for animal bravery. "She put her life on the line for Stanley, which was very noble. It just shows how far animals will go for their friends."

Stanley looks on as Dotty receives a blue ribbon for her heroism.

SEEING-EYE HORSE

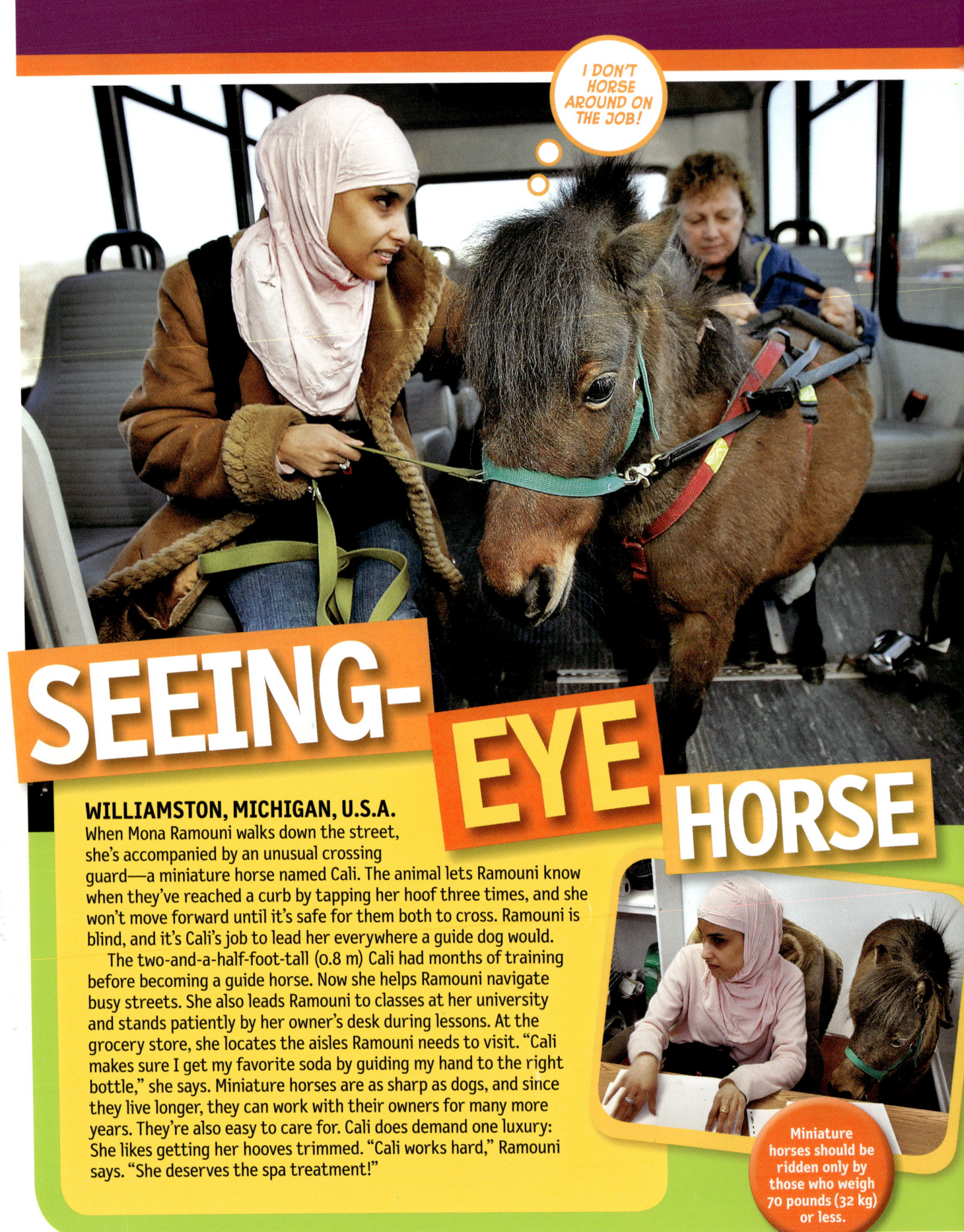

I don't horse around on the job!

WILLIAMSTON, MICHIGAN, U.S.A.
When Mona Ramouni walks down the street, she's accompanied by an unusual crossing guard—a miniature horse named Cali. The animal lets Ramouni know when they've reached a curb by tapping her hoof three times, and she won't move forward until it's safe for them both to cross. Ramouni is blind, and it's Cali's job to lead her everywhere a guide dog would.

The two-and-a-half-foot-tall (0.8 m) Cali had months of training before becoming a guide horse. Now she helps Ramouni navigate busy streets. She also leads Ramouni to classes at her university and stands patiently by her owner's desk during lessons. At the grocery store, she locates the aisles Ramouni needs to visit. "Cali makes sure I get my favorite soda by guiding my hand to the right bottle," she says. Miniature horses are as sharp as dogs, and since they live longer, they can work with their owners for many more years. They're also easy to care for. Cali does demand one luxury: She likes getting her hooves trimmed. "Cali works hard," Ramouni says. "She deserves the spa treatment!"

Miniature horses should be ridden only by those who weigh 70 pounds (32 kg) or less.

CAT FLASHES GOLDEN SMILE

Most cats can keep their coats clean themselves, but Persian cats have such long, thick fur that it can become matted unless their owners brush and groom them daily.

ALEXANDRIA, INDIANA, U.S.A.
Sebastian the Persian cat carries his bling with him wherever he goes, but this flashy feline didn't always have such a showy smile. Born with his two front teeth outside his mouth, Sebastian had a cat's face and a bulldog's smile. Owner David Steele, a dentist, worried that over time the protruding teeth would cause problems for Sebastian. Steele could have simply covered the teeth with protective porcelain. In the end, he chose another, more elegant, solution—gold crowns to cover his cat's troubled teeth! Sebastian patiently kept still while Steele used a soft, pasty material to create a molded impression of the cat's teeth. A lab used this model to make the protective crowns. Then, a veterinarian helped Steele install them. While Sebastian's teeth still stick out, now they gleam with gold!

DOG SWALLOWS 111 PENNIES

NEW YORK, NEW YORK, U.S.A.
When Jack the Jack Russell terrier jumped onto a desk to steal breakfast leftovers, he got a pile of bagel crumbs—with a side of pennies. Tearing open the bagel wrapper to get to the food, he accidentally toppled a box of coins and gulped down 111 pennies with the crumbs.

Later, owner Tim Kelleher noticed that Jack was sick and rushed him to the vet. X-rays revealed the metal meal in his tummy. Coins contain materials that are harmful to dogs if eaten, so Jack's doctors knew they had to act fast. After giving the pooch sleeping medicine, they inserted a tube with a camera at the tip through his mouth into his belly. Using the camera to guide them, staff scooped out the pennies a few at a time with a net attached to the tube.

"I've seen dogs that ate one or two coins but never this many," says veterinarian Amy Zalcman, who treated the pup. "Jack may have eaten the coins out of curiosity—and because he has a big appetite." Luckily the pooch healed quickly and went home the next day. "Now he's on a penny-free diet," Kelleher says.

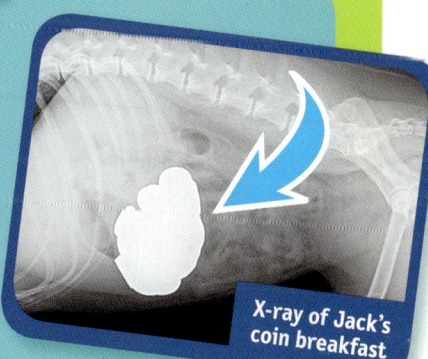

X-ray of Jack's coin breakfast

CAT RUNS FOR MAYOR

A Morris supporter holds up campaign flyers.

XALAPA, MEXICO

Fat-cat politicians beware! There's a new *cat*-idate for mayor. Supporters of Morris, your average Mexican house cat, launched a *fur*-ious campaign to have him elected as leader of the city and its 400,000 people. Tired of high crime rates and unhappy with the current crop of mayoral candidates, owner Sergio Chamorro thought his black-and-white cat might offer a *purr*-fect alternative, even though Morris sleeps a lot and doesn't do much. If voters cast their ballots based on cuteness, Morris would win "paws down."

A cat named Stubbs actually was elected mayor of Talkeetna, Alaska, U.S.A., in 1997 and was still the honorary mayor in 2013.

DOG WALKS ON "HANDS"

LOS ANGELES, CALIFORNIA, U.S.A.
Move over, circus performers. Jumpy the dog is in town! Balancing on his front paws, Jumpy, a four-year-old border collie/heeler mix, winds his way through a series of cones set out by owner Omar von Muller. A veteran performer on TV shows and music videos, Jumpy makes it look easy. It took him six months to master walking on his front legs. This superdog knows over 100 separate tricks, from riding skateboards to climbing walls. Makes you wonder, is there anything this dog can't do?

Border collies are used worldwide to herd sheep.

HORSE WORKS MAGIC

Magic (right) with her buddy Aladdin

OCALA, FLORIDA, U.S.A.
When Magic the miniature horse first visited an elderly woman who hadn't spoken in three years, the two-foot-tall (0.6 m) mare trotted right over and rested her head on the woman's lap. "Isn't she beautiful?" the woman said, shocking everyone. Thanks to Magic, she hasn't stopped talking.

Magic is a therapy horse. She visits people who have health problems to make them feel better. "Everyone always gets excited by how tiny she is," says Magic's owner, Debbie Garcia-Bengochea. "She gives people love and attention and helps take their minds off their worries."

The pint-size horse rides in cars and takes the elevator to see patients. She nuzzles up to people who can't move around well and has even sported a tuxedo for a hospital patient's tea party. "She's a small horse," Garcia-Bengochea says, "but she leaves people with big smiles."

A miniature horse weighs 15 to 25 pounds (6.8–11.3 kg), on average, at birth.

CAT GETS SWIMMING LESSONS

I wonder if the Olympic swim team needs a new member.

Right after his accident, Mog wore bandages to protect his paws.

Mog practices his strokes with his trainer.

Although most domestic cats don't like water, the rare Turkish Van cat loves to swim.

LOSTWITHIEL, ENGLAND, U.K.
When most cats get wet, the fur starts flying. Not Mog. This fearless feline doesn't mind taking dips in the pool, especially since his regular swim sessions help him grow stronger.

Owner Veronica Ashworth enrolled Mog in hydrotherapy to help the cat heal after he was struck by a car. Hydrotherapy involves low-impact exercises in warm water to strengthen muscles. The treatment has been used for humans, horses, and dogs—but rarely for cats.

"No one thought Mog would take to it," Ashworth says. "But pretty soon he was swimming laps around the pool."

Now Mog spends about 15 minutes every week gliding through the water with a trainer by his side. Slowly his front legs are getting stronger. Plus he's developed a pretty impressive swimming style. "I call it the Moggie-paddle," Ashworth says.

HALF ZEBRA, HALF DONKEY

DAHLONEGA, GEORGIA, U.S.A.

When Pippi was born, her owners naturally expected a donkey. After all, that's what her mother is. But her striped legs suggested a different kind of animal: a zedonk—half zebra, half donkey! In the wild, different species do not breed, and it's rare in captivity. "Donkeys and zebras have been living together here for years without breeding, so Pippi was a big surprise," says C. W. Wathen, founder and manager of the Chestatee Wildlife Preserve. "When I saw her little striped legs that night, I thought something was wrong with the flashlight."

Zebra, donkey, or both, Pippi's donkey and camel friends just seem to like Pippi for Pippi. She's smart and stubborn like a donkey, usually outsmarting anyone trying to wrangle her. And she "barks" like a zebra. Says Wathen, "My wife often wonders if her donkey mama knows what she's talking about."

I'M ROCKIN' THIS STRIPED LOOK.

POOCH PAINTS PICTURES

WICOMICO, MARYLAND, U.S.A.

Sammy, a foxhound/shepherd mix, is a canine Picasso. Owner Mary Stadelbacher saw a video of some dolphins that had been taught to paint and thought, "My dog can do so much better." She created a special paintbrush Sammy can grip easily in his mouth and trained him to apply paint to paper. Now after years of practice, his paintings are sold around the world. Some "fetch" up to $1,700 apiece!

Sammy is a service dog. Service dogs help people who have problems with mobility. They are trained to do things like retrieve dropped keys and pull refrigerators open.

STOOSH THE PET SKUNK

RUGELEY, ENGLAND, U.K.
How many skunks do you know that live like royalty? Stoosh the skunk rules the roost in her home. She rests her head on a plush pillow and eats fruit, nuts, and chicken from a pink bowl labeled "princess."

"She is definitely one spoiled skunk," says her owner, Dale Preece-Kelly. Stoosh enjoys leash walks with the family dogs, lounges on the couch, and snuggles in bed at night with Preece-Kelly's daughter, Mimi.

Stoosh makes her royal den under the kitchen sink. She likes to sneak things in there, like cat toys, towels, cat beds, and even sofa cushions. Once Preece-Kelly caught her dragging a full basket of laundry to her den. "Stoosh is daddy's girl and gets away with everything," he says.

Stoosh is part of her owner's traveling pet therapy operation, Critterish Allsorts. She visits homes, hospitals, and prisons, providing comfort and making people laugh.

But at home, Stoosh is 100 percent pampered pet. "Sometimes she pushes under my pillow and sleeps there all night," says Preece-Kelly. "Then I wake up in the morning with a skunk-tail mustache!"

A skunk's smelly spray can travel as far as ten feet (3 m) and linger for days.

SOCCER COLLIE SCORES GOALS

OCALA, FLORIDA, U.S.A.
He shoots! He scores! BEK the soccer-playing border collie attacks the ball with his open mouth, dribbles it with his nose, and dazzles the waiting goalies with his speed. Named after soccer champ David Beckham, BEK understands that his job is to put the ball in the net. And he usually succeeds—even against professional goalies.

Owner Mark Lukas created the humans versus canines soccer game after watching a border collie race across the field dribbling a ball at a soccer match. After playing against hundreds of humans, his Soccer Collies now travel all over North America. They perform at halftime shows, visit schools, and entertain at fairs and festivals. "BEK is probably the best soccer dog in the world," Lukas says. "He's obsessed with the game. He would rather play soccer than eat!"

Soccer probably originated in China, in a game called Tsu Chu in the third to second centuries B.C. when the game involved kicking a leather ball stuffed with fur.

WORLD'S OLDEST PIG

GARLAND, TEXAS, U.S.A.
Why would 100 people attend a party for a pig? To celebrate his being the oldest potbellied porker on the planet, of course! In July 2013, Potsie turned 21 years old and seemed to enjoy celebrating his special birthday. "He wagged his tail and sniffed people," says owner Maria Grieser. He feasted on his favorite foods—raisins and apple slices. In fact, he "pigged out." Even the town's mayor came to pay his respects. Now that's one pig worth oinking about!

Potbellied pigs can be trained to walk on a leash and use a litter box.

8 REAL ANIMAL HEROES!

Would an animal care enough to save another creature's life? Some experts say absolutely not. But these heartwarming stories of pet heroism seem to tell a different tale.

1 DOG RESCUES KITTEN

ANDERSON, SOUTH CAROLINA, U.S.A.
Animal control officer Michele Smith heard the cry for help and climbed down the steep embankment. Nobody knows how Goldie the shih tzu mix and Kate the kitten ended up together, trapped at the bottom of a deep ravine behind a hardware store. But one thing's for sure: Goldie wasn't going to let that kitten die. She nursed the baby, protected her, and barked like crazy until help arrived. Smith carried the pair to safety in a makeshift sling, digging her fingernails into the dirt to climb out. Once at the animal shelter, Goldie groomed the kitten and carried her around in her mouth. "Goldie is Mama," says Randi Leigh Knox, who works at the Anderson County P.A.W.S., a nonprofit organization dedicated to caring for stray and abandoned pets. "She may be a dog, but when I have kids, I hope I'm half as good a mother as Goldie."

Chinese royalty kept shih tzus as prized house pets for more than 1,000 years.

2 DOG SAVES KID FROM TRUCK

CLACTON, ENGLAND, U.K.
Geo the German shepherd mix follows ten-year-old Charlie Riley everywhere. When Charlie plays on his trampoline, Geo scrambles up a rock and jumps beside him. When Charlie sits on the couch, Geo cuddles close. Naturally the pup goes along on family walks.

One day Charlie, his mom, and his two younger brothers were standing at a street corner. Geo was sitting at Charlie's side. Suddenly, "we hear a roar," Charlie's mom says. An out-of-control pickup jumped the curb. It was heading straight for Charlie! But Geo made a flying leap. "He hits me so hard I fall over," Charlie says. The speeding truck slammed into Geo instead, knocking him out of his harness. The driver kept going, but two bystanders ran over to help. They rushed Geo to the animal hospital, where vets performed emergency surgery.

"My dog could have died," Charlie says.
And my son could have, too, thinks his mother.
But he didn't—thanks to Geo.

Geo is all bandaged up in this photo, but today he's just fine.

3 CAT RESCUES COUPLE

MOUNT GILEAD, OHIO, U.S.A.
Tiger the stray cat didn't look like a hero. He showed up scrawny and flea-infested at Rod and Michelle Ramsey's house. Unable to turn away a hungry face, they took him in. Three years later, the couple were in bed with blinding headaches. Suddenly Tiger burst into their room and howled. "I've never heard such a noise," Michelle says.

When Tiger wouldn't stop, Michelle stumbled down the hall and let him outside. That's when she saw her older cat staggering and called the vet. Veterinary assistant Julie Higgins answered the phone. "You have carbon monoxide poisoning," she said when she heard Michelle slurring her words. "Call 911 and go outside!" Carbon monoxide is a deadly gas. Invisible and odorless, it was leaking out of the Ramseys' heating system.

Paramedics arrived. An emergency helicopter airlifted the Ramseys to the hospital. Doctors pumped oxygen into their lungs, and they both survived. All thanks to a cat no one else wanted.

4 FELINE DEFEATS ROBBER

MIAMI, FLORIDA, U.S.A.
Homer the blind cat weighs only four pounds (1.8 kg). Gwen Cooper adopted the little stray when he was three weeks old. Because of an eye infection that left him blind, he would have been euthanized if she hadn't taken him in. Homer never lets blindness stop him. "He's a bold little adventurer," Cooper says. "He's fearless." The cat proved this one night when his growling woke up Cooper. He'd never growled before. Surprised, Cooper opened her eyes. A burglar was standing at the foot of her bed! Cooper reached for her phone to call 911.
"Don't do that!" the intruder said. The sound of his voice pinpointed his exact location, and blind Homer leaped. No match for a snarling cat with extended claws, the would-be robber fled.

5 PUP DETECTS SEIZURES

LAS VEGAS, NEVADA, U.S.A.
Zoe the pit bull mix is Gretchen Jett's best gift ever. Born deaf, the 11-year-old girl also has epilepsy, a brain disease that causes seizures. Because of this, she usually has to play indoors. So one day her dad got a dog to keep her company. Just two nights later, Zoe burst into Gretchen's parents' room when they were asleep. "She's acting strange," Gretchen's dad remembers. "I get up, thinking she needs to go outside." Instead, Zoe ran in a circle and bolted straight into Gretchen's room. Gretchen was suffering a bad seizure. Circling and running became Zoe's signal. "When she does that we know something is wrong with Gretchen," her dad says.
Not bad for an untrained dog that came from a shelter. Zoe's previous owner couldn't keep her because the rambunctious mutt kept running away. That's not a problem now. Why? Because Zoe knows that Gretchen needs her.

6 PUP SAVES TEEN FROM FIRE

WEST JORDAN, UTAH, U.S.A.

It was three in the morning, and a mother and two children huddled outside in their pajamas as firefighters hosed water on their burning house. "Is anybody inside?" the firefighters asked.

The mom thought that perhaps her older son had escaped out the back, but just to be sure, Don Chase and his partner plunged through the flames to look.

And what did they find? Teddy the toy poodle standing by the door. Chase reached for him, but the pup scooted down the basement stairs. Midway down, he stopped and waited. But just as the firefighters reached him, he took off again. "I'm really irritated," Chase remembers. "We're wasting time chasing a dog when we should be searching for human victims."

Then they saw him—the older son unconscious on a basement couch. Grabbing his legs and chest, the astonished firefighters hauled him to safety, as his devoted dog trotted behind.

"That dog risked his life for the kid," Chase says. "If I hadn't seen it, I wouldn't have believed it."

7 KITTY DEFENDS POOCH

MIDDLETOWN, RHODE ISLAND, U.S.A.

Bert the tabby cat and Lili the pug aren't friends. "They basically ignore each other," says owner Gary Paquette. But when Lili needs help, it's the cat that comes to her aid.

It was still dark outside early one morning when Paquette opened their sliding glass doors to let Lili out. Their yard is fenced in, so Paquette sat down inside to wait. Soon Bert joined him. But the cat barely got settled before he rose up on his hind legs, leaned his paws against the glass, and growled. Paquette wondered what was going on. He grabbed a flashlight and stepped out on the deck. There in his flashlight beam was a yellow-eyed coyote standing on his dog! Paquette ran screaming into the yard. Startled, the coyote jumped the fence.

Lili needed stitches and antibiotics but recovered quickly. It's lucky for her that Bert's ears were tuned in. The animals' owner didn't hear a thing.

8 CAT DETECTS LOW BLOOD SUGAR

EDMONTON, ALBERTA, CANADA

Monty the orange tabby cat didn't appeal to Patricia Peter at first. She really wanted a kitten. But all the kittens at the Humane Society had already been adopted, and the Siamese she liked was ignoring her. So Peter adopted Monty.

Six months later, she was asleep when Monty bit her hand. "It's the hand I poke to test my blood sugar level," she says. Peter has diabetes, a serious disease that requires frequent blood testing. Wanting to sleep, Peter pushed the cat away. But Monty only bit harder. Finally Peter got up. Monty led her to the kitchen and jumped on the counter beside the testing kit.

Guess what? Peter tested, and her sugar level was dangerously low. She popped some sugar pills, and her level returned to normal. According to Peter's doctor, Monty knew something was wrong by smelling her breath and tasting her skin.

"He's my guardian angel," Peter says. Chances are Monty feels the same about her.

JUST WAIT TILL I ACTIVATE MY eBAY ACCOUNT.

NAUGHTY DOG BUYS STUFF

RICHMOND, VIRGINIA, U.S.A.

Christine Payne and Greg Strope had a mystery to solve. An email confirmed a $62.50 purchase of 5,000 Xbox points. The problem was they hadn't bought a thing. They searched for clues and found the game controller on the floor, covered with bite marks and dried slobber. Also at the scene was a likely suspect: Oscar the dog.

Turns out Strope had left the tempting controller on the coffee table, and Oscar, a hound/Labrador retriever mix, couldn't resist. He chewed until he turned on the video game and clicked through the screens, accidentally buying points on the system. "He was a puppy, so he would chew anything he could reach: shoes, clothes, paper," Payne says. In the end, the video game company refunded the money and, just for fun, set up the pooch with his own screen name: Oscar the K9.

Dogs chew on objects to keep their teeth clean and their jaws strong, to relieve boredom or anxiety, and as a way of exploring the world.

FLORIDA THE TURTLE

Three-toed box turtles are named for having three toes on their hind feet.

PLANTATION, FLORIDA, U.S.A.
Florida the three-toed box turtle doesn't move very fast, but he's got mad skills! He flips over onto his back on command and then he rolls back upright again. He can also stay and heel like a dog and "chase" his tail—although it takes him a minute or two to do one lap. He'll even give a high five! But doing tricks isn't Florida's only job. He helps owner Dr. Mitch Spero, a psychologist, by getting his younger patients to "come out of their shells" with a little laughter. Florida mastered his tricks over a ten-year period—"turtle time" as Spero calls it. Still, with his reptile brain, "for him to remember anything and repeat the tricks is remarkable," Spero says.

MICROCHIP LOCATES LOST CAT

FRIENDS FURR-EVER!

ROHNERT PARK, CALIFORNIA, U.S.A.
A tiny computer chip about the size of a grain of rice helped reunite Jackie Sharp and her long-lost cat, Dallas, after 13 years apart. When Dallas was a kitten, he had been implanted with a computer microchip that held contact information for his owner in case he ever went missing. One day in 2000, Dallas wandered off by a nearby stream—and never returned. Sharp searched for the cat but couldn't find her pet anywhere. Years went by and no one called to say they had found Dallas. Sharp moved several times, and she never stopped wondering about Dallas. Then in spring 2013, someone found the cat near the same creek where he had disappeared years earlier and took him to an animal hospital. There the vet noticed the microchip implant under Dallas's skin and immediately called Sharp to tell her the pet had been found. When they were reunited, Dallas recognized his owner right away and hopped into her arms after 13 years!

Millions of microchips have been implanted in pets worldwide.

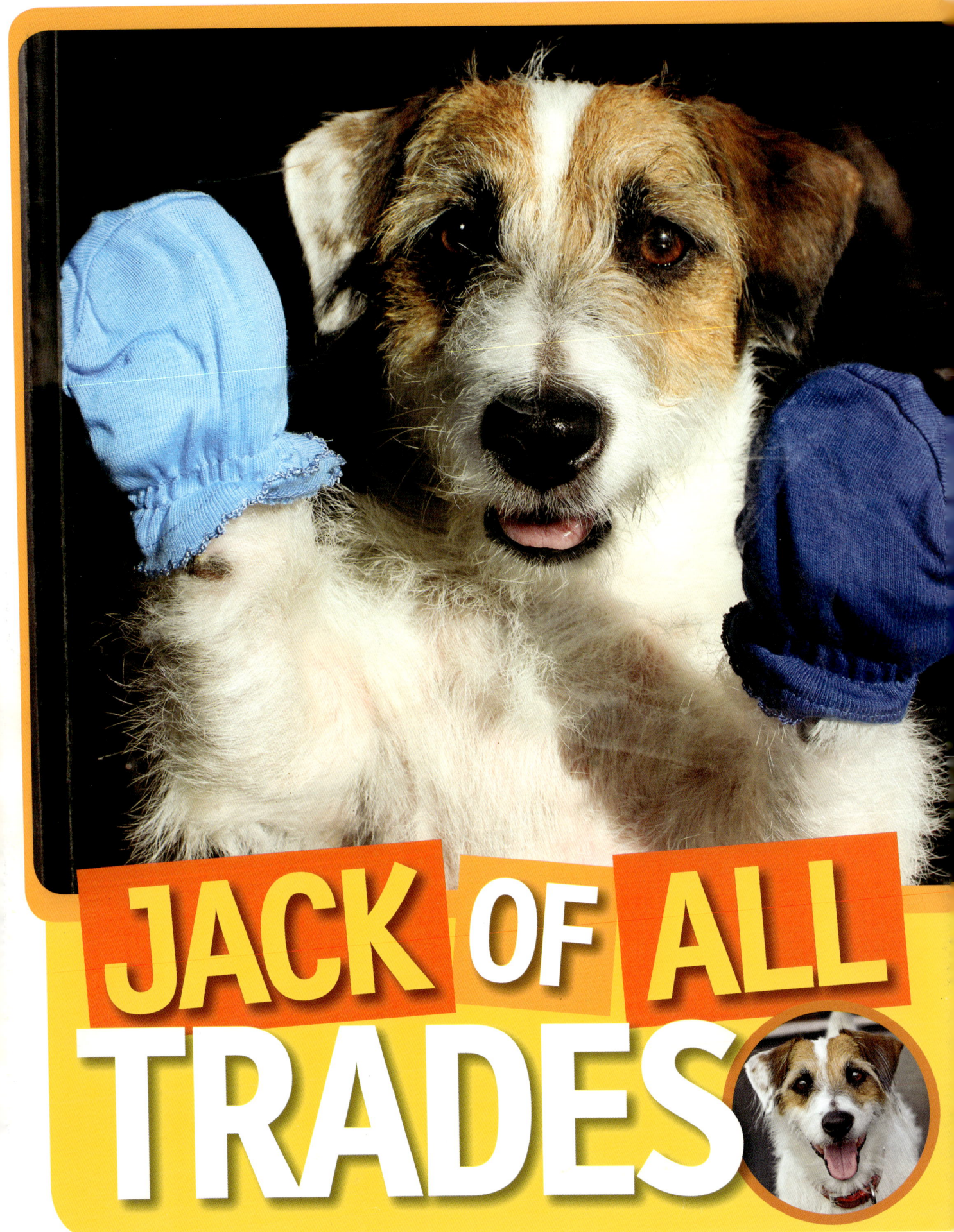

JACK OF ALL TRADES

Jack Russell terriers were bred for hunting small animals underground and love to chase, explore, and dig.

WHO SAYS HOUSEWORK HAS TO BE RUFF?

LITCHFIELD PARK, ARIZONA, U.S.A.

Jesse the Jack Russell terrier pops frozen pancakes in the toaster, brews coffee, and even sets the table for his owner, Heather Brook. After breakfast he helps with household chores like vacuuming, wiping up spills, picking up trash, making beds, fetching the newspaper, and checking the mail. It all started when Brook got Jesse as a puppy for her 16th birthday. "When he was nine weeks old, he taught himself how to stand up and beg like a meerkat," says Brook. "Then we started working on more advanced tricks." Jesse even knows how to untie his owner's shoes at night and give her a back rub. "Jesse is a big ham and will do anything to get a laugh," Brook says. One time she wasn't laughing: when he chomped down a little too hard on the television remote he was delivering to her—oops!

NOM NOM NOM …

DOG BOTTLE-FEEDS SHEEP

DEVON, ENGLAND, U.K.

When Jess the springer spaniel is on sheepherder duty, she doesn't just guard her herd—the pooch bottle-feeds members of the flock! Carrying a milk-filled container with her mouth, Jess dashes to the herd's orphaned lambs and patiently holds the bottle as they each take a drink.

According to owner Louise Moorhouse, Jess learned to feed the young sheep all by herself. "One day she just picked up a baby bottle off the ground and the lambs began guzzling from it," Moorhouse says. "Jess has been bottle-feeding the lambs without moms ever since." Now Jess brings milk to her woolly charges three times a day. "It's hilarious to watch her bound around with the bottle in her mouth, dripping milk along the way," Moorhouse says. When the pooch isn't making deliveries, she's checking on the flock and giving them cleanings by licking their faces.

So why is this sheepherder so eager to provide lambs with milk? "Like humans, dogs do things they find rewarding," dog behavior consultant Pat Miller says. "Caring for the lambs must make Jess one happy pooch."

When she's not busy bottle-feeding sheep, Jess is extra helpful, carrying equipment and buckets of feed around the farm for her owner.

HAMSTER ROBOT PILOT

DIXON, CALIFORNIA, U.S.A.
Who puts the "ham" in "ham-bot"? Princess the hamster! When animator and robotmaker I-Wei Huang engineered a machine to be powered by a hamster, he asked his nieces Gracie and Daisy Ballance if their pint-size pet could serve as a test pilot. "Our uncle made this crazy hamster-ball walking thing," says Gracie. Turns out Princess was the perfect fur ball to power it up. "She got in the ball and ran superfast," says Daisy. Princess was a pro right from the start, supercharging the robotic walker with every paw-pounding plastic twirl. Go, Princess, go! At one point, she ran so fast, she almost powered the robot right off the table.

Females of some hamster species stuff their young into their cheek pouches when they sense danger.

PANDA COW

COVINGTON, WASHINGTON, U.S.A.
No, you're not seeing things—this cow is a panda. Or is this panda a cow? Named Amazing Grace, she "is the result of several breeds of miniature cattle with very distinctive characteristics," says Michelle Gradwohl. Her father, professor Richard Gradwohl, has worked for 35 years to perfect the cuddly black-and-white bovine breed. Amazing Grace's wide, white belt makes her one of very few perfectly marked panda cattle in the world. But this barnyard pet cares a lot more about having fun than about her looks. Amazing Grace loves kicking up her heels in the pasture and chasing butterflies. She also loves being pampered. "Every day, she wants to be brushed and scrubbed under her neck," Michelle says. It's for real—this cow is *bear*-y much a part of the family.

Panda cattle are bred primarily as pets.

JUST CALL ME SQUEALS ON WHEELS!

PIG HAS WHEELS FOR LEGS

SUMTERVILLE, FLORIDA, U.S.A.

Chris P. Bacon the potbellied pig is always ready to roll—literally. Born with malformed hind legs, the animal has a set of wheels that can be attached to his back end to help him move.

The orphaned piglet received his ride after being adopted by the family of veterinarian Len Lucero. "When Chris P. Bacon first came to live with us, he struggled to walk," Lucero says. "We wanted to make things easier for him." So the animal's owners used a toy building set to make him a miniature pig-mobile: a brace made of short plastic rods that connects to a small seat between two wheels. Gently strapped into the brace with his rump on the seat, he could use his forearms to pull himself forward while his back legs rolled along. In no time, Chris P. Bacon was cruising around his home. Later, Lucero found a company to make a sturdier metal ride for the pig.

Now Chris P. Bacon spends time chasing toads and taking walks with his owners. Once he's tuckered out, Lucero removes the wheels so the pig can get some rest. Says Lucero, "This pig loves napping as much as roaming."

DOG RUNS ON CROSS-COUNTRY TEAM

Guide dogs are trained to follow a clear path, negotiate around obstacles, and stop at curbs.

MANSFIELD, OHIO, U.S.A.
When she hears the word "run," Chloe the golden retriever does the happy dance, then slips into her harness and gets to work. She's a guide dog for her blind teenage owner, Sami Stoner. With Chloe's help, Sami competes on her high school's cross-country team. The sport involves running long races over natural terrain.

"Before Chloe, I fell all the time just walking on the sidewalk," Stoner says. "With her at my side, I have a lot more confidence."

Running through the woods, Chloe guides her girl along the path, navigating around fallen branches and creeks. At school, Chloe leads the way through crowded hallways and snoozes during class. Chloe's so popular that she was crowned homecoming queen along with her owner. "Chloe wasn't too happy about wearing a crown. She kept knocking it off," Sami says. "But I think she enjoyed being a little queen!"

PARROT SAVES TODDLER

DENVER, COLORADO, U.S.A.
"Mama, baby! Mama, baby!" When babysitter Meagan Howard heard those words coming from Willie the parrot, she knew something was terribly wrong. Howard was in the bathroom when her pet bird started screeching. She ran to see what had happened and discovered two-year-old Hannah Kuusk choking on food and turning blue. Thinking quickly, she performed the Heimlich maneuver and dislodged the snack.

"Willie calls me Mama, and he knew Hannah was in trouble," Howard says. "He wanted me to help her." Parrot expert Phoebe Greene Linden says that parrots—very brainy birds—can sense scary situations. "They develop strong bonds with humans and are highly aware of change, even danger," she says. Today little Hannah is healthy and happy—and Willie won't let her out of his sight. "He follows her wherever she goes and squawks, 'I love you,'" Howard says. That's one devoted parrot!

There are approximately 350 species of parrots worldwide.

DOGS DRIVE CAR

Ginny at the wheel

AUCKLAND, NEW ZEALAND

Ginny, Monty, and Porter don't hang their heads out of the window during a car ride—these rescue dogs are too busy driving. After two months of learning how to operate a vehicle, each pooch was able to steer an automobile around a racetrack.

"We wanted to prove how smart rescue dogs are," animal behaviorist Mark Vette says. Vette first used voice commands and treats to teach the pups how to turn a steering wheel and move a lever to shift car gears. Then the trio practiced their new skills in custom-made karts.

Soon the dogs were ready to hit the road in an actual car. Modified with special features, the pooches' ride accelerated only up to 7.5 miles an hour (12 km/h), and trainers could stop the auto by using a remote control. The dogs took turns getting strapped into a safety harness in the driver's seat. Then, following the voice commands of caretakers just outside the vehicle, each pooch shifted a lever to put the car in drive, slowly turned the wheel to steer around the course, and pulled another lever to brake. Wonder if they'll be flying planes next.

DOUBLE-DUTCH DOG

LONG ISLAND, NEW YORK, U.S.A.

Geronimo the Australian cattle dog mix holds the world record for double-Dutch jump rope. When she hears the slap of the jump ropes, she barks like crazy. She waits for the ropes to be in just the right position and then—*boing!* She jumps in and jump, jump, jumps—once bouncing 114 double-Dutch skips in a row to set the Guinness World Record. "She loves it," says her owner, dog trainer Samantha Valle, who adopted Geronimo as a puppy. "As long as I have food, she'll work forever." Nicknamed "Mo," this pup is a jumping maniac, making appearances all over the country showing off her double-Dutch skills. This hobby also keeps Mo out of trouble. If she gets bored, she chews everything in sight. Keep jumping, Mo, or you'll end up in the doghouse!

Double Dutch is a jump rope skipping game that involves turning two ropes in opposite directions, like egg beaters.

CAT RUNS FOR SENATE

I HOPE THERE ARE MICE IN CONGRESS.

SPRINGFIELD, VIRGINIA, U.S.A.
The claws came out during 2012's elections—one of the candidates running for office was Hank the cat.

With his owners' help, Hank was campaigning to be a U.S. senator. The cat's name wasn't actually on the ballot (voters could write him in), so his caretakers didn't expect him to win. "But by running, Hank [drew] attention to issues like the value of animal shelters," owner Matthew O'Leary says.

The 13-pound (5.9 kg) politician visited pet stores to meet supporters, attended photo shoots, and even appeared in his own campaign ad. To look spiffy on the campaign trail, he wore a plaid tie and regularly got his nails trimmed. But Hank's bid for a spot in the U.S. Senate didn't get in the way of his favorite activity. "He still [got] plenty of nap time," says O'Leary.

Hank's Senate campaign raised $60,000 for animal rescue organizations.

KID POWER

A male goat is called a buck; a female goat is called a doe.

COMSTOCK PARK, MICHIGAN, U.S.A.
Prince the goat might have died without help from Sara Manley. She bottle-fed the furry five-pound (2.3 kg) orphan, dressed the tiny kid in baby pajamas, and snuggled him to sleep at night. But as Prince grew, Manley realized that the little goat was helping her, too. "At three weeks of age, Prince could detect my low blood pressure and seizures," she says. He would nudge her, scream, and walk in circles around her a few minutes before a seizure, giving her a chance to take her medicine to prevent the seizure from happening. It wasn't long before Prince was certified as an official service goat. He wears a vest and escorts Manley wherever she goes. "His calm and steady demeanor makes him perfect for the job," Manley says. "Not all goats are cut out for it." How does Manley repay Prince for all of his hard work? "He gets lots of love," she says. Plus all the animal crackers he can eat—paper box and all.

I DON'T MEAN TO BE CATTY, BUT I AM ONE PURR-TY FASHION MODEL.

Orion the cat models his Hawaiian beachwear at the feline fashion show.

CATS BECOME MODELS!

NEW YORK, NEW YORK, U.S.A.

Dressed up like a tourist in Hawaii, Orion the cat strutted his stuff. As he struck a pose, he was joined by ten other fashionable felines strolling down the runway. The cats made perfect models during the Feline Fashion Show at New York City's famous Algonquin Hotel. The event raised $2,000 for North Shore Animal League America and also celebrated the 13th birthday of the hotel's resident cat, Matilda, who greets hotel guests from her plush chaise lounge in the lobby. As Matilda watched the show, Max prowled by dressed in denim duds, and Kashmir twirled in a ballerina costume. Elvis the Savannah cat even shook up the runway twice, first in a white spangled jumpsuit and then in a black leather biker jacket. Was that Elvis meowing the loudest when everyone sang "Happy Birthday" to Matilda at the show's end?

Elvis

Safram Hale Bop

Max

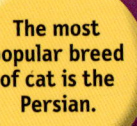
The most popular breed of cat is the Persian.

THREE-LEGGED JUMPING GOAT

Tumbleweed's long toenails help him balance.

MUSKEGON, WISCONSIN, U.S.A.
Tumbleweed the pygmy goat leaps the fence at Godsell Farm and races to greet his owners. Not so amazing? Well, it is for a goat with three legs! Tumbleweed did not have enough room in his mother's womb, say owners Mark and Pam Godsell, and as a result, he was born missing a leg. At first, the Godsells had to prop him up so he could nurse from his mother, but eventually he learned to balance on his own. From then on, there was no stopping the determined little goat. Tumbleweed can jump higher than any other goat on the farm. In fact, the Godsells had to make the fence higher to stop him from leaping away!

DOG RUNS ROAD RACE

FULTON, MARYLAND, U.S.A.
When 2,000 runners raced past his yard, Dozer the goldendoodle couldn't resist joining the fun. For eight miles (12.9 km), this champion athlete pounded the pavement with people raising money for cancer research. At the 13.1 mile (21 km) marker, Dozer dashed across the finish line, barely out of breath. "Runners were taking pictures throughout the race," says his owner, Rosana Panza. Volunteers reported the dog lapping water from paper cups at the water stations, too. The race organizers awarded him a finisher's medal and set him up with his own website. Since then, Dozer has raised more than $30,000 for the cause—more than any human competitor!

The goldendoodle was originally bred to obtain a dog with a nonshedding coat for people with allergies.

DOG SCOOTERS KITTY

Are we there yet?

ORANGE COUNTY, CALIFORNIA, U.S.A.
With a hop and a push, Rogue the Australian cattle dog jumps on his scooter and takes his friend Lynxie the cat for a ride. "Rogue figured out how to coast," says the dog's owner, Linda Wright. "It's a nice ride, but he's the worst about stepping on the cat." Lynxie doesn't seem to mind, even hanging on when Rogue jumps off the scooter and sends his feline friend for a crash landing. The one-year-old dog learned to scooter as a pup. He also pushes a baby carriage, plays dead on command, and drives a toy tractor. "He pushes the gas pedal and loves to honk the horn," Wright says. That's just how he rolls.

The Australian cattle dog was bred to control groups of wild cattle through the Australian wilderness.

RAT BIRTHDAY PARTY

Pet rats usually enjoy having their ears rubbed.

NEW YORK, NEW YORK, U.S.A.
For Vinnie the rat's first birthday, his owner, Dianne Rochenski, threw him a birthday bash to make sure her new pet felt loved and spoiled. "All of his brothers and sisters celebrated with him," says Rochenski. For the big event, she dressed the whole pack of ten rats in their finest attire. Her female rats wore sparkly, ruffled dresses with polka dots. She dressed pink-eyed Vinnie in a shiny, blue "big boy" tuxedo. Party-goers nibbled on potato chips and cupcakes. Why go all out for a rodent's birthday? Rochenski says: "Because my boy is worth it."

PARROT CLUCKS LIKE CHICKEN

QUIT STEALING MY LINES.

The blue-fronted Amazon parrot gets its name from the bright blue feathers on its forehead, above the beak.

PRENTON, ENGLAND, U.K.
When Jack the blue-fronted Amazon parrot returned home after going missing for two cold months, his relieved owner got a surprise. The chatty parrot opened his beak and started clucking like a chicken!

Experts think that Jack probably bunked at a farm, sharing food, water, and warmth inside a henhouse. "Amazons are amazing at learning sounds of the forest, other animals, or human voices," says bird expert Steve Farro of the National Aviary in Pennsylvania, U.S.A. "The parrot was probably hanging with chickens and learned their sounds." Jack also can mimic a smoke alarm and a television theme song, says owner Jerry Williams, but these days he sounds like a parrot ... mostly. "He does his chicken impression whenever he feels like showing off," Williams says.

DUCKS MARCH ON!

MEMPHIS, TENNESSEE, U.S.A.
Each morning at 11:00, Duckmaster Anthony Petrina leads his five feathered friends through the lobby of the Peabody Hotel. Guests laugh and cheer as the ducks proudly parade across a red carpet to the magnificent marble fountain. There they swim and play until 5 p.m. They feast on cracked corn and pose for photos with hotel guests. A few "duck divas" try to get in all the photos, says Petrina.

At the end of the day, the ducks march out, again to loud applause. They spend their evenings in a $200,000 Royal Duck Palace on the hotel roof. Their room overlooks the city. They swim in a bronze fountain and eat food served by a butler.

Petrina trains the ducks, which are wild, to march to and from the fountain. "Ducks are about as smart as cats and easier to train," Petrina says. After three months of service, the ducks are released back into the wild, and five new ducks get trained. For three months, though, the Peabody ducks are "flying high"!

FLYING GUINEA PIG

Guinea pigs are no longer found in the wild.

ROSYTH, SCOTLAND, U.K.
It's a bird! It's a plane! No, it's Truffles, the jumping guinea pig! After reading through *Guinness World Records* for guinea pig records, owner Chloe Macari wondered if Truffles might be able to break the record for jumping. She put Truffles on one shoebox, and a cucumber (his favorite treat) on another shoebox a few inches away. He immediately leaped to reach the treat.

As Truffles's jumping skills grew, Macari gradually moved the boxes farther apart. Truffles officially set the world record in February 2012. He jumped 30 cm (just under a foot) in front of a cheering crowd at a local scout hall. After that, he broke his record two more times.

He jumped 48 cm (about a foot and a half) in April 2012. Even when he's not training, Truffles continues to practice. "He often jumps around his cage and even jumps over our other guinea pig," Macari says. The sky's the limit for this high-flying guinea pig!

TORTOISE TAKES LONG WALKS

MANCHESTER, ENGLAND, U.K.
Maximus the tortoise and owner Rob Davies stroll through their neighborhood for up to five hours a day. Davies says the long walks are healthy and enjoyable both for him and for Maximus. Plodding along at a top speed of one mile an hour (1.6 km/h), Maximus gets his exercise while Davies hardly breaks a sweat. Even the gawking neighbors and the honking cars don't stop this tortoise from "racing" to the finish line. At birth, Maximus fit in the palm of Davies's hand. Four years later, he weighs over 25 pounds (11.3 kg) and eats more than 70 pounds (31.8 kg) of lettuce weekly. That's a lot of salad! But he sure works off some of that food through his daily walk. "Slow and steady wins the race," goes the old saying. If that's true, Maximus and Davies are winners every day.

BUNNY HOP!

The Netherland dwarf rabbit weighs about as much as eight sticks of butter.

JENA, GERMANY

A white-and-black blur, Snoopy bounded over one hurdle after another. The smallest rabbit in the jumping competition, the Netherland dwarf raced through the obstacle course, clearing hurdles that many larger rabbits couldn't. Before retiring in 201 Snoopy competed in jumping events across Europe, often finishing among the top three.

One time on a German television show Snoopy cleared a 55-cm hurdle (about 22 inches). This was three and one half times Snoopy's height. That would be like a six-foot-tall (1.8 m) human athlete jumping more than 20 feet (6 m) high

Snoopy loved to compete, say owne Michael Zuerch and Sara Gerstner. "Spectators loved him for being the smallest of all and trying so hard and defeating even much bigger-breed rabbits." He often ran the training course on his own without urging. He didn't seek any reward or treat other than being praised and petted. After a successful competition, he came looking for Gerstner to lick her hand and nose.

ONE FINE FERRET

CHICAGO, ILLINOIS, U.S.A.
Mr. Binky the ferret reigned supreme at ferret shows. Over three years, he competed in ten shows across the United States, winning at least one first-place ribbon in each. He even earned the title of national Companion Ferret of the Year in 2010.

Mr. Binky had everything judges seek in a ferret: a well-shaped head, clean teeth and ears, trimmed nails, a smooth coat, and a slender, muscular physique, says owner Pamela Hines. His friendly personality also made him a judges' favorite. To prepare for a competition, Hines washed and groomed Mr. Binky and cleaned his teeth (using chicken-flavored toothpaste). She also made sure he exercised. Climbing helps build the muscles the judges look for, she says.

While Mr. Binky liked traveling and meeting different people, he is now enjoying a well-earned retirement. "He still comes out of his cage to play," says Hines. "He just takes longer naps now." Maybe sometimes he also sneaks a peek at his array of ribbons, which Hines always has on display.

Ferrets sleep 18 to 20 hours a day.

DOG BECOMES ARCHAEOLOGIST

WONDER IF I'LL FIND AN ANCIENT CHEW TOY.

BRISBANE, AUSTRALIA
Migaloo the dog has a real nose for history. She's known as the world's first canine archaeologist, using her powerful sniffer to find buried ancient remains.

"The work is like a game for Migaloo," owner Gary Jackson says. "When she arrives at an archaeological site, she immediately begins smelling the soil for bones." The four-year-old pooch trained for six months to prepare for her job and was rewarded with a game of fetch whenever she made a discovery. Now Migaloo regularly joins excavation teams to search for remains of Australia's first inhabitants, the Aborigines. The pup's coolest find? Bones that were 600 years old buried six feet (1.8 m) underground!

"Dogs have at least 125 million receptors in their noses that pick up scents—humans only have 5 to 10 million," dog expert Stewart Hilliard says. "This supersensitive schnoz makes dogs like Migaloo great for archaeological work." Migaloo also has some cool moves. "When she makes a find, she does a shimmy," Jackson says. "It's her victory dance."

> Sheep can recognize faces of other sheep and remember them for up to two years.

SHEEP TAKES WALKS WITH DOGS

TORRINGTON, ENGLAND, U.K.
Heads always turned when Scarlett Wise went out for a walk with her family's dogs ... and Tinkerbell the lamb! Trotting along on her own leash, Tinkerbell fit right in. According to owner Chiara Magarotto, the lamb sometimes even seemed to think she *was* a dog.

Tinkerbell was born small and weak with poor eyesight and brain damage. It wasn't clear if she would even survive. But when Magarotto brought Tinkerbell home, her daughter Scarlett immediately bonded with the tiny lamb. Born prematurely, Scarlett had spent weeks in the hospital as a baby. She insisted they try to save the lamb.

Tinkerbell didn't just survive. She became part of the family, which included four dogs, other sheep, cats, retired racehorses, and a chicken. She enjoyed tea parties with Scarlett. Most of all, she enjoyed her walks with the family's dogs. There were always lots of barks ... and a few *baa*s.

PUP SCOUT

NEW YORK, NEW YORK, U.S.A.
Tasha Bella the Manhattan morkie and nearly 30 of her dog pals frolic together in a New York City park. This is no regular puppy play day. It's a meeting of Pup Scout Troop 4. For the occasion, Tasha wears a dress fashioned after a Brownie uniform. The dress features badges Tasha has earned, as well as a matching brown cap. A pampered pooch, Tasha has more than 200 outfits. The Pup Scout uniform is a favorite, though.

Each Pup Scout meeting begins with owners reciting a special pledge on their dogs' behalf: "On my honor, I will try to do my duty to help the dog community and my country, to help make humans smile, to be there to guard and protect, especially those at home."

"The dogs like bonding with their owners and playing with their friends," says Tasha's owner, troop leader Susan Godwin. The Pup Scouts earn badges for activities such as painting (with paws), showtime (doing tricks), and "doga" (owners doing yoga with dogs). Dogs also earned a pink ribbon badge for participating in a cancer awareness walk. If they go camping, we know where they'll sleep—in a pup tent!

A morkie is a mix between a Yorkshire terrier and a Maltese.

Cooking badge

ROOSTER STRUTS IN BOOTS

WOODSTOCK, NEW YORK, U.S.A.
Flipper the rooster sure is stylish in his boots, but he wasn't always that way. Flipper started limping soon after he was brought to Woodstock Farm Animal Sanctuary in fall 2010, and the owners concluded that he had circulatory problems. His toes soon turned black, and in no time, they fell off! All he had left were short nubs, but that didn't stop Flipper. He learned how to walk without toes, but because he had a hard time keeping his balance, the workers gave him baby socks and dog boots. "It didn't take him long to get used to the boots," says sanctuary manager Sheila Hyslop. Flipper had his strut back, not to mention he was the sharpest-dressed animal on the farm!

A rooster in a dark room will still know it's dawn and time to crow!

SHADOW THE DOG SOARS

THIS IS MY GAME FACE.

Hang gliders fly at speeds ranging from 16 to over 100 miles an hour (26–161 km/h).

SALT LAKE CITY, UTAH, U.S.A.
Shadow the Australian cattle dog and his owner, Dan McManus, do everything together—even hang glide! Strapped into a special harness, Shadow calmly takes in the bird's-eye view as the wind whips by. You may be wondering how a dog picks up such a daredevil hobby. Well, it was actually Shadow's idea. McManus has been hang gliding for more than 30 years, and one day as McManus ran to get airborne, Shadow followed, nipping at his heels and then grabbing on and going airborne for a few feet. It was then that McManus decided Shadow should ride along with him. Now, Shadow is a pro. He's more than man's best friend—he's man's best copilot!

OTTER LOVES DOGS

WHAT? I MAY LIKE TO PLAY WITH DOGS, BUT I DON'T HAVE TO SMELL LIKE 'EM.

DARIEN, GEORGIA, U.S.A.
Dogs play together all the time. But dogs and an otter? That's unusual.

Ootie the river otter was brought to SOS Wildlife Resources after he was injured by a car. While he recovered, Chelsea the golden retriever and Donor the bloodhound entertained him, touching noses through his outdoor cage. After three weeks, the otter was released back into the river.

But guess who waddled out of the water two days later? Ootie! Chelsea and Donor were so excited that they ran to the river's edge to greet the otter. Then Chelsea waded in. "Ootie swam circles around her," says sanctuary director Nan Page. When he was done having fun, Ootie swam away, back to his wild life.

Ootie visits often to play tag with Chelsea, Donor, and another dog named Bowbie, or just to snuggle with them under some shade. Page, who avoids contact with the otter to keep him wild, says otters are usually afraid of dogs, and dogs are natural predators of otters. "But these guys are too busy playing to know that," she says.

The river otter is a member of the weasel family.

OWL RIDES DOG

CORWEN, NORTH WALES, U.K.
Most barn owls fly from place to place, but Willow preferred to hitch a ride on the back of best buddy Merlin. When Willow finished her daily exercise at Pen y Bryn Falconry, handler Lorwi Peacock placed her on the back of Merlin as he prepared for his walk. Surprisingly, both owl and dog enjoyed the odd pairing. As Merlin trotted along, Willow held tight with her claws and spread her wings to keep her balance. Merlin may not be magical like the wizard from the King Arthur tale, but he's still pretty special to Willow.

A barn owl has such an acute sense of hearing that it can locate prey hidden under snow.

FLUFFY BULL

ADEL, IOWA, U.S.A.
You wouldn't expect people to call a 1,500-pound (681 kg) bull named Texas Tornado "cute," but when photos of the fluffy bull went viral in 2013, he soon became a fuzzy celebrity. People have been breeding fluffy cows and steers for years, but more and more people are falling in love with these stylish cattle. Owners can enhance the animal's fluffiness through daily washing and drying.

"Texas Tornado likes getting bathed with soap and water," says owner Matt Lautner. "He also likes it when you comb him. He'll always chew his cud, which is a sign of satisfaction in cattle."

Being fluffy has other benefits besides just looking stylish. The fluffy hair helps keep cattle warm in the winter. In the summer, "they shed their hair so that they can stay cool and comfortable," says Lautner. Comfort and style—Texas Tornado has them both. And that's no bull.

YOU KNOW YOU WANNA PET ME.

Blow-drying a cow to look fluffy can take over an hour.

DOG WEARS WIGS

I'M READY FOR MY CLOSE-UP!

The Bedlington terrier has a woolly coat that can resemble a lamb's.

BAY HARBOR ISLANDS, FLORIDA, U.S.A.
Simon the Bedlington terrier loves all the attention he gets because of his pink wig. Made from the same synthetic fiber as many human wigs, the featherlight hairdo attaches under Simon's chin with an elastic band, allowing his floppy ears to hang free. Ruth Regina, an eighth-generation wigmaker (for humans) and owner of Wiggles Dog Wigs, has created many popular styles, including an Elvis Presley look. "What a darling thing for dogs to wear," Regina says. "It brings a lot of happiness to people, and the dogs love it, too." What's next? Regina thinks Simon might look good in dreadlocks!

DOG MOTHERS TIGER CUBS

CANEY, KANSAS, U.S.A.
In July 2008, a white Bengal tiger mother at the Safari Zoological Park abandoned her cubs, Nasira, Sidani, and Anjika, just one day after they were born. They would not survive without milk, but fortunately zoo owners Tom and Allie Harvey had a pet golden retriever named Isabella that had just finished weaning her puppies. That meant she was still able to make milk and could be a substitute mom. "As soon as she saw them, she licked the tiger cubs as if they were her own pups," say the Harveys. "They immediately took to nursing." The puppies and cubs played together as one happy family, and the tigers have since grown up to be quite big (they celebrated their fifth birthday in July 2013). Isabella still drops by to visit from time to time.

White Bengal tigers are extremely rare, especially in the wild.

FAMOUS GOAT

HOULTON, MAINE, U.S.A.
Other goats at Took a Leap Farm relaxed in the sun, but not little Buttermilk. She had lots of energy to burn off. The five-week-old Nigerian dwarf goat ran in circles around her friends. Sometimes she leaped over them as if they were obstacles on a course. Owners Kathryn Harnish and Rob Lawless thought Buttermilk's antics were cute. Harnish posted a video on the Internet. Soon Buttermilk had gone viral. A year later, nearly ten million people had watched the video.

Whenever Harnish takes Buttermilk out into the community, people crowd around to see the famous goat. Buttermilk is even getting her own video game!

A group of goats is called a trip.

COCKATOO MAKES TOOLS

VIENNA, AUSTRIA
Figaro the Goffin's cockatoo is raking in the snacks—literally. When the bird spots food lying just out of reach of his cage, he builds a tiny wooden tool to sweep the tasty prize his way.

The bird first revealed his talent when a pebble he was playing with rolled out of his cage. The cockatoo's leg wasn't long enough to reach the stone. So he flew away and returned with a twig, slipping it through the fence to slide the pebble toward him.

Scientists at the University of Vienna, where Figaro lives, were excited—the bird had used a tool, something cockatoos don't usually do. Wondering if he would do it again, they placed a nut exactly where the pebble had been. This time, Figaro used his beak to carve and pull out a small strip of wood from a beam in his cage. He then dragged the nut toward him with his new rake.

Although many animals use rocks or sticks as tools, few create them as Figaro did. "Now he can make a tool in five minutes," says researcher Alice Auersperg, who studies Figaro. "It proves that he has very good problem-solving skills." Who knew supergeniuses came with feathers?

I'M CUCKOO FOR CASHEW NUTS.

6 Silly Pet Tricks

Just training a dog to roll over is no easy feat, but these amazing pets have been taught to perform some extraordinary tricks. Check out these cool critters!

THESE PETS LIKE DOING TRICKS, BUT YOUR PET MAY NOT. NEVER FORCE YOUR PET TO DO A TRICK IT DOES NOT WANT TO DO.

I'VE GOT NINE LIVES, RIGHT?

1 CAT WALKS ON BALL

CHICAGO, ILLINOIS, U.S.A.

Why won't you see Jax the cat's pawprints on the floor? Because the kitty can move from place to place on a large, rolling ball! The feline propels the ball forward by walking on top of it. "Jax has always loved perching on narrow surfaces, including my shoulder," owner Samantha Martin says. "I thought she'd like even cooler balancing acts." To prepare for the trick, Jax practiced standing on a smaller ball set in a bowl so it couldn't move. Then Martin placed her on a bigger ball at one end of a short track. On the other end were yummy cat treats. The clever kitty quickly figured out that if she carefully inched backward on the ball, she could move it down the track—and get her delicious reward.

Around 1876 in Liège, Belgium, cats were trained to deliver mail.

Goats bleat with different accents in different environments.

2 GOAT COASTS ON SKATEBOARD

FORT MYERS, FLORIDA, U.S.A.

Jumping on her skateboard, Happie the goat zips down driveways and cruises along sidewalks. The animal first showed her zeal for wheels when she tried to leap on her owner Melody Cooke's bicycle. Cooke decided to get Happie her very own skateboard and train her to ride. After a lot of practice and goodies, the goat learned some sweet boarding moves: She could stand on the board, give a big push-off with her hind leg, and roll forward. "Sometimes Happie became unsteady and had to jump off," Cooke says. "But she always got right back on." Now Happie can coast for more than a hundred feet (30.5 m) without stopping. Talk about being on a roll.

MACAW TAKES UP SKIING

3

CANNES, FRANCE

Luna the hyacinth macaw loves to fly—down a ski slope! Owner Mark Steiger knew the eight-year-old bird would be a natural skier. "Hyacinth macaws like Luna have strong legs," he says. First, Luna practiced walking while clutching handles on tiny skis with her claws. Then Steiger taught her to slide down a custom-made four-foot-tall (1.2 m) slope on the skis, rewarding Luna with treats at the bottom. The macaw even learned to take a "ski lift" up her slope. With her hardy beak, she grasps onto a metal ring that Steiger uses to pull her up the slide. Just before Luna whooshes back down, she leans forward like a competitive skier. "She picked that up all on her own," Steiger says. "Luna's a total pro."

HERE GOES NOTHIN'!

The hyacinth macaw's wingspan can be nearly as long as an eight-year-old person is tall.

4 PIG JAMS ON HORNS

FRANKTOWN, COLORADO, U.S.A.
Mudslinger the pig is a real hog when it comes to music. He enjoys creating tunes with horns, and once he gets started, he sometimes doesn't want to stop. Trainer John Vincent introduced the pig to the horns by tooting some in front of him. After watching his owner, the curious pig tried squeezing the instruments with his mouth to make noise. Whenever he continued, Vincent fed him juicy grapes to keep him motivated. "Now Mudslinger comes up with his own songs," he says. Each time the curly-tailed rock star jams on his horns, he'll toot them in a different order to create a new pattern of sounds. "His favorite horn in the set is the deepest, loudest one," Vincent says. "He likes to end his performances with it."

Mother pigs may "sing" to their young while nursing them.

5 SID THE SHOW DOG

LAS VEGAS, NEVADA, U.S.A.
You've got to hand it to Sid the Aussie cattle dog—she can perform a handstand on her owner's palm! According to Lou Mack, the talented pup will try just about any trick if it means getting to play with her favorite toy afterward. "Sid's a real Frisbee nut," Mack says. To conquer the handstand, Sid was positioned upside down with her front paws in Mack's hand and her hind paws pressed against a wall. Soon the dog's leg and back muscles became so strong she could hold herself in the handstand without any support. "For Sid, this is just fun," Mack says. "She looks happy all the time—even when she's upside down."

About 78 million pet dogs live in the United States—that's one for every four people.

6 HORSE PLAYS B-BALL

BOCA RATON, FLORIDA, U.S.A.
Before he makes a slam dunk, Amos the miniature horse looks around to see if people are watching. "Amos definitely likes an audience," owner Shelly Mizrahi says. To teach him to play basketball, Mizrahi gave Amos carrot slices each time he touched his nose to a hoop set on a short stand. Later, Amos learned to pick up a small ball with his teeth and place it in the hoop. Scoring baskets has become the horse's all-time favorite activity. The hoofed athlete once dunked the ball a hundred times in a row. "Amos can also paint and play a xylophone with a mallet," Mizrahi says. "But if I place a paintbrush, a musical instrument, and a basketball in front of him, he always goes for the basketball."

Some early miniature horses were bred as pets for kings and queens.

WORLD'S TALLEST HORSE

Big Jake raises money for good causes by appearing at county fairs and festivals.

POYNETTE, WISCONSIN, U.S.A.

Big Jake towers over his owner, Jerry Gilbert, at nearly 6 feet 11 inches (2.1 m) tall from hoof to shoulder. That's about as tall as an NBA basketball player! He even holds the Guinness World Record as the tallest horse on the planet. Big Jake has a big appetite, too. The 12-year-old Belgian draft horse eats a bale and a half of hay and 30 quarts (33 L) of oats each day. "He likes for people to scratch his neck and head," says Gilbert—if they can reach that high.

LIZARD LIVES LARGE

Mostly found in Africa and Asia, monitor lizards can grow up to ten feet (3 m) in length.

BUDD LAKE, NEW JERSEY, U.S.A.
It's what owner Dominic likes to call a "spa day" for Bandit. First he carries the six-foot (1.8 m) monitor lizard out to the front yard of his house. There Bandit gets to "tan" outside while he walks around the yard on a leash. Next the brown-and-yellow lizard gets washed with soapy water and scrubbed down with a brush. After Dominic dries Bandit off with a towel, he checks between the lizard's toes for dead skin. Then he trims the lizard's nails and rubs his ears. "I want to make sure he's happy, healthy, and clean," says Dominic about his scaly friend.

This pampered lizard is really part of the family. Even Dominic's two-year-old daughter shows no fear. She smiles at Bandit and holds his tail. This "lounge lizard" lives a lucky life.

POOCH SAVES FAMILY

BEWARE OF DROOL.

HILLSBORO, OHIO, U.S.A.
Hercules the Saint Bernard didn't take long to say "thanks" to his new family for adopting him. The pooch had been at his home for just six hours when he saved his owners from being robbed.

The canine's caretakers had put Hercules in the backyard to play. Immediately, the dog sensed something was wrong: He noticed a burglar trying to break into the basement. Growling, the dog leaped off the back porch and bolted toward the intruder. The thief began running with Hercules bounding behind. The dog chased the robber until the man disappeared over the backyard fence.

"Saint Bernards are known for being helpful," says Karen Bodeving, president of the Saint Bernard Club of America. Still, Hercules' family is amazed by how quickly the dog became loyal to them. Says owner Lee Littler, "He's earned a lifetime of treats."

DUCK FASHION SHOW

NEXT UP: AMERICA'S NEXT TOP WADDLE.

DENILIQUIN, AUSTRALIA
Sarah the duck isn't afraid to strut her stuff on the catwalk. The stylish bird is part of an annual just-for-fun duck fashion show. She kicks off each show by appearing in a pink gown with a cape as toe-tapping music plays in the background.

During the show, Sarah and other ducks from her farm sport superfancy bird-size gowns and suits. The colorful outfits, which wrap around the birds and snap to close, are custom designed by a tailor. They're also comfortable. "All the clothes are soft and have holes for wings," owner Brian Harrington says.

To prepare for the event, the ducks practice walking in their elegant getups at their farm. When it's showtime, the feathered fashionistas waddle a few at a time down a miniature runway. Wearing everything from frilly frocks with matching hats to stylish vests, the birds wow the crowds. "They get a lot of applause and everyone wants to take their picture," Harrington says. Those are some lucky ducks!

Sarah commands the catwalk.

Nakala (left) and Fay sport matching getups.

A different Sarah (left) and Gill are stunning in magenta.

DOG FLIES AWAY

ROCHESTER HILLS, MICHIGAN, U.S.A.
Tinkerbell the Chihuahua was relaxing with her owners at an outdoor market when a 70-mile-an-hour (113 km/h) blast of wind tore through the area. Tables and chairs flew into the air—and so did the six-pound (2.7 kg) Tinkerbell. Her frantic owners chased after her, but the wind carried her away like a furry paper airplane.

For two days owners Lavern and Dorothy Utley searched the area. But the only sign of Tinkerbell was her leash, found about a quarter of a mile (0.4 km) away. Desperate, the Utleys wandered along an old trail, calling the dog one final time. She came running!

No one is sure how Tinkerbell survived her windy ordeal—or her landing. "She was probably only six or eight feet [1.8–2.4 m] off the ground," meteorologist Dave Rexroth says. "I suspect she was tossed around like a tumbleweed until she got caught in small trees." Her owners, however, don't care how she managed to survive. "We're just tickled to death to have her back," Lavern says.

I MUST HAVE A LITTLE BIRD DOG IN ME.

CAT RESCUES OWNER

STURGEON BAY, WISCONSIN, U.S.A.
It was nighttime and very quiet, but Pudding the cat sensed trouble in his home. His owner, Amy Jung, has diabetes—a condition in which the body can't control blood sugar levels. While asleep, Jung's blood sugar had dropped so low she began to have a seizure and then went into a coma. If she didn't get her medication soon, she could die.

Somehow Pudding knew his owner was in danger and sprang into action. Leaping onto Jung's chest, he frantically swatted her face with his paw to wake her. When she didn't stir, the usually gentle cat nipped his owner's nose. Jung came to but couldn't move or speak. So the cat dashed off to alert her eight-year-old son, Ethan. "I have no idea how Pudding got into his room because the door was shut," she says. After the cat woke the boy, they rushed to Jung, and Ethan gave her medicine.

"Cats like Pudding form strong bonds with people and want to help if something goes wrong," says cat behaviorist Mieshelle Nagelschneider. Jung has recovered but is still in awe of Pudding. "I'm so lucky to have this big, fuzzy lifeguard around," she says.

A THANK-YOU BELLY RUB? YES, PLEASE!

DOG RIDES SCOOTER

Speed limit? What speed limit?

CANTON, GEORGIA, U.S.A. Forget walking. When Norman the briard wants to get around, he's got a much snazzier form of transportation. The pooch has been riding his family's scooter since he was a puppy. "One day we put him on the scooter and wheeled him around for fun," owner Karen Cobb says. "He didn't want to get off."

Cobb and her kids trained Norman to ride the scooter much like a human would ride one. Propping his front paws on the handlebars, the dog stands on the scooter's board with one back paw and propels himself forward with the other.

Norman rolls around the neighborhood with Cobb by his side making sure he's safe. "The second we take out the scooter, his tail starts wagging," she says. But Norman soon may be ready for some new wheels: He's learning to ride a bike!

Norman takes his scooter out for a spin.

CAT TAKES *TRIP*

PALM BEACH GARDENS, FLORIDA, U.S.A.
When Gracie Mae the cat spotted an open suitcase, she did what many cats do: She hopped inside and burrowed under the clothes. Never realizing she was inside, owner Seth Levy closed the suitcase and headed to the airport. That's when Gracie Mae's adventure began. Still in the suitcase, the cat went through an x-ray machine and into the plane. She flew from Florida to Dallas, Texas, then shot down the ramp into baggage claim, where the wrong passenger picked up the suitcase. Finally, nine and a half hours later, a hungry, cranky Gracie Mae escaped from the luggage—to the surprise of the other passenger, who quickly called Levy's wife, Kelly. "She was back to her affectionate self the next day," she says. These days, Gracie Mae flies in a carrier. After her adventure, she must feel as if she's flying first class.

AT LEAST THE CLOTHES IN THE SUITCASE WERE CLEAN.

Cats like crawling into boxes and suitcases because it makes them feel safe and protected.

DONKEY HEROES

WITH THOSE EARS, HOW COULD THEY NOT HEAR MY WHINNIES FOR HELP?

Virginia (front) and her foal Violet

FREDERICK, MARYLAND, U.S.A.
Curly, Charlotte, and Jennifer the donkeys knew something was wrong. Virginia the pony was about to have a baby, but she had fallen on her side and couldn't get up. Panicked and thrashing, the pony risked hurting herself—or her foal.

The donkeys dashed to their owners' farmhouse, braying like a crazy donkey alarm. "When I heard all three of them, I came running," owner Lisa Carr says. She quickly delivered Virginia's foal but couldn't get the terrified 1,000-pound (454 kg) pony up. Once again, the donkeys sensed danger. While Curly stayed behind to lick and comfort the newborn, Charlotte and Jennifer rushed back to the house to alert Carr's husband.

Soon the two humans got Virginia back on all four hooves, and she began to nurse her foal. "Donkeys look out for their herd, and Virginia is part of that herd," says agriculture expert Jon Gersbach. Carr agrees. "Curly, Charlotte, and Jennifer are like the very best watchdogs ever."

TALK ABOUT MEOW MIX!

CAT HAS TWO FACES

SOUTH FLORIDA, U.S.A.
This is one two-faced cat. Venus's unique mug is divided down the middle—one side is jet black, while the other is light orange.

Why does Venus have such a dramatic look? Every animal's body contains sets of genes passed down from parents. These microscopic molecules determine how the animal will look, including the color of its skin, hair, and fur. "It's possible that the genes that decide fur color came together in an unusual way in Venus," cat researcher Leslie Lyons says. "This may have led to her odd coloring."

Even though Venus doesn't look like a regular cat, she sure acts like one. The mischievous kitty enjoys sneaking chow from the dogs' bowls and scampering after toys. And according to Venus's owner, the feline gives lots of cuddles and kisses. Who wouldn't want face time with this cool cat?

Venus's eyes are two different colors as well. Green or yellow is typical for cats. Experts think Venus's genes also caused one of her eyes to be blue.

CHIHUAHUA CHASES AWAY BURGLARS

ALTADENA, CALIFORNIA, U.S.A.
Paco the Chihuahua was curled up for a snooze in his neighbor's shop when two masked men burst through the door. They charged toward the counter, shoved an empty bag at the cashier, and ordered him to fill it with money.

Awakened by the noise, Paco leaped into action. The pint-size pooch bounded toward the intruders, barking loudly and nipping at their ankles. Startled, the robbers took off running. But Paco wasn't done patrolling. The ten-pound (4.5 kg) security guard followed the thieves outside and chased them down the street before returning to the shop.

What turned this normally calm and friendly pet into a feisty crime fighter? Veterinary behaviorist Terry Marie Curtis thinks Paco actually might have been scared when the robbers entered the store. "Sometimes when animals are frightened, they act aggressively to make the scary thing go away," Curtis says.

Whatever Paco was feeling, everyone in the neighborhood was impressed with his bravery. "He's a real superhero," shop owner Erik Knight says. "All he's missing is a little cape."

COCKATOO BEATS THE ODDS

FORT LAUDERDALE, FLORIDA, U.S.A.
Oscar the "naked" cockatoo may not be the prettiest bird around, but she (yes, Oscar is a girl) may be one of the most loved. When Oscar came to the Broward County Humane Society 17 years ago with beak and feather disease, experts thought she had only a few months to live. Oscar has not only survived but she has also become a local celebrity. "When she's in front of a crowd, she puts on a show," says Cherie Wachter of the Humane Society. "At first people are taken aback by her appearance, but she soon wins them over with her personality." Oscar has since left the hubbub of a public living space to move in with Humane Society employee Lorna Inge. Oscar seems to enjoy the quiet—she laid 13 eggs in one year (after laying just one in all her years at the Humane Society). She even started to sprout some feathers. Oscar continues to defy the odds!

CAMEL DINES WITH OWNERS

ASHBOURNE, ENGLAND, U.K.

Joe the Bactrian camel is *way* too fancy to have breakfast in his stable. Instead, the fine diner eats morning meals with his caretakers at the kitchen table.

"The first time Joe showed up for a bite, we definitely weren't expecting him," says owner Nathan Anderson-Dixon. The animal had been grazing in his pasture when he smelled food cooking. Following his nose, he trotted up to the house through an unlocked gate, poked his head into an open kitchen window, and gently plucked a morsel of food from the table with his lips.

Now Joe is a regular visitor at breakfast. His favorite treats are cereal and toast topped with bananas. At first his owners weren't sure they wanted the humped guest dining with them. But they've grown fond of his daily appearances. "Joe's a member of the family," Anderson-Dixon says. If only he'd learn to use a napkin.

DOG PROTECTS PIGLET

HÖRSTEL, GERMANY

When Roland Adam found an orphaned newborn Vietnamese potbellied pig alone and shivering on his farm, he wasn't sure he knew what to do. But Katjinga the Rhodesian ridgeback did. She snuggled up to the pint-size pig (now called Paulinchen), cleaning her with her tongue and nursing her as she would her own puppy. "Katjinga lay down, fed her, and kept her warm," Adam says. In fact, this wasn't the first time Katjinga cuddled up with orphaned animals—she's also tended rabbits and ducks. "Recently, we found her warming up one of our sheep that was sick," Adam says. Sounds like one protective pooch!

YOU SMELL A LOT BETTER THAN THOSE OTHER PIGS.

CAT GETS BIONIC FEET

SURREY, ENGLAND, U.K.

When Oscar the cat lost his back feet in an accident, his owners thought he'd have to be put down. Cats need their back feet for survival. But veterinarian Noel Fitzpatrick had an idea.

Fitzpatrick and a team of engineers created the first ever realistic prosthetic cat feet for Oscar. The new feet were based on the way antlers grow from a deer's head. The cat's skin and bones could grow into the prosthetics so they'd become part of his body. Rods were fused into Oscar's leg bones, then special curved "feet" were attached. (Cats rock on their feet to move themselves forward.) Finally, Fitzpatrick attached tire-like rubber to the bottom of each foot so Oscar wouldn't slip.

Today Oscar does anything that four-footed cats do, including jumping onto beds, crawling up curtains, and even scratching his ears with his plastic feet. Mice, beware: Oscar is on the prowl!

The surgery to fit Oscar's prosthetic feet took three hours.

NOW HOW ABOUT SOME HONEY?

PUPPY SAVES FRIEND FROM BEES

BEE-WARE OF DOG!

KENT, OHIO, U.S.A.

Pinky the boxer puppy sensed danger buzzing in the backyard. Nine-year-old Richie Bragg was searching for the pooch's ball when suddenly bees swarmed on his foot. "Pinky nipped my feet and barked and jumped on me," says Richie, who is allergic to bee stings. "I think she was telling me to get away."

As Pinky continued to bark and chase the bees, Richie ran inside to safety. Soon the pooch was covered in bees and stung more than 40 times. Richie was rushed to the hospital, Pinky to the vet. Both are doing fine.

Experts think that Pinky reacted to Richie's yelling and slapping after he was stung. "I'm not sure the dog was thinking, 'I'll go distract the bees,'" says Mary Burch, animal behaviorist with the American Kennel Club. "But Pinky definitely knew her little boy was in trouble."

Whatever Pinky was thinking, Richie knows one thing: "She saved me from all those bees," he says. "She's my hero."

ALPACA RIDES THE WAVES

SAN BARTOLO, PERU
Pisco the alpaca catches some waves with owner Domingo Pianezzi—and everyone on the beach stares. Pianezzi fastens Pisco into a black flotation device and places cotton in his ears in case he falls into the water. He gently carries Pisco into the ocean and helps the animal kneel on the surfboard. Then Pianezzi climbs on behind Pisco and starts paddling. Catching a wave, Pianezzi stands up. Then Pisco tries, too. On his first attempts, Pisco wobbles on his skinny legs and immediately tumbles into the water and paddles toward shore. Finally, Pisco gets upright and balances briefly on the surfboard before wiping out.

This isn't Pianezzi's first time surfing with animals. Previously, he shared his surfboard with a dog, a hamster, a parrot, and a cat. But teaching an alpaca to stand up on a surfboard may be the greatest trick of all.

KITTY CRIME SPREE

SAN MATEO, CALIFORNIA, U.S.A.
A sly thief sneaks through a neighborhood looking for loot. When he sees something he likes, he steals it and drags it away—with his teeth. The tricky four-footed suspect? Dusty the cat.

This furry offender has carried home more than 600 items over the past four years. He leaves his spoils on his front lawn or slips them one at a time through the dog door. Dusty once raked in 11 objects in a single night. He gets his goods from neighbors' yards, nabbing everything from socks and stuffed animals to gloves and goggles.

According to cat behavior expert Marilyn Krieger, Dusty's just being himself. "Some cats like collecting things," she says. "They're natural hunters, and searching for objects to bring to their families is a type of hunting behavior." The cat's most fashionable find? A pink sequined purse he brought home, just in time for Valentine's Day.

I WANT TO SPEAK TO MY LAWYER.

Dusty with a few of the goods he snatched

WANTED

THE CRIMINAL
Dusty the cat

THE CRIMES
Trespassing and robbery

STOLEN ITEMS
1 baseball mitt
21 shoes
75 socks
102 gloves
231 towels

MONKEY HELPS OUT

BOSTON, MASSACHUSETTS, U.S.A.
When Ned Sullivan needs to wash his face or untie his shoes, Kasey the capuchin monkey is there to help. If Sullivan is thirsty, Kasey will open a water bottle for him and put in a straw. She even scratches his itches!

Kasey met Sullivan, who was paralyzed in a car accident, after attending Monkey College. This school trains capuchins to assist people with disabilities. While there, she learned to load DVDs, turn book pages, switch lights on and off, and more.

Now Kasey uses her skills to make Sullivan's life easier. She's also challenging him to heal faster. Kasey makes Sullivan reach for objects and places things in his weaker hand so he can exercise it. All this has helped him regain a lot of movement. Says Sullivan, "Every day, Kasey takes me further."

WE MAKE AN AWESOME TEAM!

The capuchin monkey lives in tropical forests in parts of Central and South America.

Kasey hands Sullivan a beverage.

I'M ALL EARS.

FOUR-EARED CAT

CHICAGO, ILLINOIS, U.S.A.
People do a double take when they see Yoda the cat. That's because Yoda was born with an extra set of ears. A restaurant owner was trying to give the cat away but had no takers because of the cat's odd look. "The customers seemed almost frightened of him because he looked so weird," says Ted Rock, who adopted Yoda. "But I thought he was the cutest kitten I'd ever seen." Veterinarian James Antonicic says Yoda's second set of ears are actually just extra skin, developed when his earflaps split into two before he was born. "He can't hear out of them," Antonicic says. "It's just extra skin in a nifty spot on the top of his head." Yoda's real ears work just fine, which the family dog knows all too well. Yoda has no problem hearing when the dog gets fed and comes running to stand in between the pooch and the bowl. "Yoda loves to tease," Rock says.

THESE ARE SOME FUNNY-LOOKING CHICKS.

PUPPY-SITTING HEN!

SHREWSBURY, ENGLAND, U.K.
Whenever Nettle the Jack Russell terrier takes a break from her four pups, Mabel the chicken hustles to where the puppies are sleeping. Like a true mother hen, she fluffs her feathers and plops down on the puppies. Mabel tucks them in under her warm body as if the pups were a brood of chicks.

"At certain times, a hen will sit on anything that's warm and nest-like," says chicken behavior expert Bob Bailey. Gentle Mabel will cluck softly to her nest of "hatchlings" until their mom returns.

Mabel is a caretaker, but she's also a disciplinarian. Sometimes the puppies rambunctiously play with Mabel's feathers. "If they get too rough," says Edward Tate, the farmer who brought Mabel into the house after a horse injured the hen's foot, "Mabel gives them a glare and a gentle peck." Don't mess with this mother hen!

IT'S NOT THE MOON, BUT I'M WORKING ON IT.

COW JUMPS HURDLES

Regina and Luna spring over an obstacle.

LAUFFEN, GERMANY

Luna the cow really stands out from the herd. The bovine not only lets her 16-year-old caretaker ride on her back—Luna can also leap over hurdles.

Owner Regina Mayer decided to try "cowback riding" with Luna after learning she couldn't have a horse. She began training the farm animal by taking her for long walks. Then Regina saddled Luna and carefully rode her around. Once Luna got the hang of being ridden, she was ready for another challenge—jumping!

After months of practice and plenty of treats, the cow could leap over obstacles. Now Luna loves to show off her horselike moves and even responds to commands such as "go," "stand," and "gallop."

"Cows are intelligent animals," says veterinarian Owen Rae of the University of Florida. "With repetitive coaching and a caring trainer, they can learn to do a lot." In other words, these gals are *udder*-ly amazing.

Cows often jump into the air when they get excited.

KAI THE WOLF-PUP NANNY

SOUTH SALEM, NEW YORK, U.S.A.
Kai the German shepherd may not wear a whistle around his neck, but when it's time for the wolf pups at the Wolf Conservation Center to swim in their blue plastic kiddie pool, he plays lifeguard. On duty, the 95-pound (43 kg) pooch nannies the pups, comforting them, teaching them manners, and keeping them out of trouble. Sometimes he spends an entire morning grooming them. Kai's owner, Rebecca Bose, works as curator of the center, where pups Alawa and Zephyr live as ambassador wolves. They follow Kai around and mimic what he does—sniffing what he sniffs, looking at what he looks at, and sleeping where he sleeps. If they do something naughty, like sneaking a bone, biting Kai's tail too hard, or having too much of a howling good time, Kai uses gentle but firm body language to say "no." When Kai's off duty, this über-working pet gets bored. "At home, he looks at me as if to say, 'Can we get back to work here?'" Bose says. Lucky for Kai, he also nannies geese and ducks!

German shepherds are used as the world's leading police, guard, and military dogs.

SPOILED SWINE

RUSHLAND, PENNSYLVANIA, U.S.A.
Wilma the potbellied pig receives royal treatment at a special spa for swine. She relaxes in the grooming room with calming music and a lit candle—just like in many human spas. First, the "pigtician" gives Wilma a cleansing shampoo and shower, scrubbing off any remaining mud and dirt with a toothbrush. Then, using oils, she offers an energy-releasing massage treatment. The finishing touch is a squirt of cologne to make Wilma smell fresh and clean. The process leaves pigs "quiet and relaxed," says farm owner Susan Magidson. And as if that isn't enough, then it's time to do what pigs do best ... why, "pig out" of course! There's a tasty meal of grains, cucumbers, carrots, and apples waiting for Wilma before she beds down in her comfy stall. That's some spoiled swine!

Some pigs are afraid of mud.

HORSES ROAM THE HOUSE

IS THERE ROOM FOR ME?

AYRSHIRE, SCOTLAND, U.K.

No need to leave a key under the mat for Lucien and Amigo. These two horses can get into owner Sharon Taylor Bastable's house without one. Each horse knows how to push the front door handle down with his mouth until he hears the click. Then he nudges the door open with his nose and strolls inside. Both horses just like to "hang in our company," says Bastable.

Sometimes the horses get into mischief. Lucien used to come in when the family had visitors and help himself to cookies. Another time Bastable heard a clunking noise coming from her son's room when she knew he was outside. She peeked inside and saw Amigo tossing her son's shoe around the room with his mouth. When Amigo saw her, he dropped the shoe and stopped for a moment. But soon he resumed his game.

Still, Bastable and her family always welcome their houseguests. After all, everyone enjoys a little "horsing around" with friends.

These horses even give the family cat, Sampson, a lift around the house!

FURRIEST FELINE

Himalayan/Persians are people-friendly and enjoy cuddling in their owners' laps.

HOLLYWOOD, CALIFORNIA, U.S.A.

Salute Colonel Meow! With fur measuring nine inches (23 cm) long, this Himalayan/Persian crossbreed holds the Guinness World Record for longest fur on a cat. The famous feline, rescued from a shelter, has even appeared on *Good Morning America*, say owners Anne Marie Avey and Eric Rosario.

How did Colonel Meow get his name? "With his piercing stare and prominent frown, I thought he needed a rank," says Avey. She began posting photos and videos of her furry friend, and soon the Colonel became an Internet star. Seeing Colonel Meow online, Guinness contacted Avey about the possible record. A vet took fur samples, and two witnesses also verified the length.

To keep the Colonel's long fur under control, Avey gives him a thorough brushing twice a week. Even so, she finds fur "on the couch, on the bed, and in the car." The Colonel may look gruff, but underneath his scowl he's sweet and gentle, says Avey—a real pussycat!

RABBIT THINKS SHE'S A LEOPARD

WHAT SHOULD WE DO NEXT? AND DON'T SAY HOPSCOTCH.

HODENHAGEN, GERMANY

Lisa the rabbit definitely has a wild side—sometimes she acts more like a big cat than a bunny. Playing chase with her leopard pal, Paulchen, Lisa zooms after her friend and then, bam, goes in for a playful pounce!

Zookeepers at the Serengeti Park, where the animals live, had placed the rabbit and leopard cub in the same enclosure to keep each other company. The two quickly became buddies, and Lisa started acting like a leopard. Her favorite game was to pretend-hunt her much larger pal. She scampered after Paulchen and leaped onto him, or sneaked up a table and tackled him from above. "I've seen felines play like this, but not rabbits," says keeper Jessica Hamza. "It was funny to watch her behave like a cat."

As both animals grew, the leopard moved in with his own species and Lisa joined two monkeys. "Now she acts like the monkeys," Hamza says. "They climb around together and groom each other." This little friend sure knows how to fit in.

CAT WAITS FOR TRAIN

MELBOURNE, AUSTRALIA

Graeme the cat doesn't hang out at home waiting for his owner, Nichole O'Duffy, to return from work at the end of the day. Instead, he heads to the train station to meet her.

"One day Graeme just showed up," says O'Duffy, who adopted the cat from a friend. Now he sees his owner off each morning and returns for her in the evening. As he waits, the feline enjoys pats from other commuters. When the train pulls in and the doors open, he sits patiently behind the yellow safety line.

Experts can't completely explain Graeme's behavior. "Cats possess superb memories and like having a routine," veterinarian Amber Andersen says. "But Graeme's story is extraordinary." Wonder if he makes airport pickups, too.

A calico cat named Tama serves as honorary stationmaster at a Japanese railway station.

ALL ABOARD!

The platform is Graeme's hangout hot spot.

Tom Bennett and his dog Brody, a five-year-old goldendoodle, ride on a Jet Ski on Pigeon Lake near Bobcaygeon, Ontario, Canada. Bennett says Brody, who is known as Goggle Dog on Pigeon Lake, has fallen off his Jet Ski once. He didn't like it much, but he doesn't hesitate to hop aboard and ride the waves. The goggles keep dragonflies from hitting him in the eyes.

Index

Boldface indicates illustrations.

A
Adam, Roland 95
Airplanes, horses flying in 24, **24**
Alawa (wolf) 101, **101**
Alpacas 97, **97**
Amazing Grace (cow) 55, **55**
Amigo (horse) **102**, 103, **103**
Amos (miniature horse) 85, **85**
Anastasi, Donna 17
Andersen, Amber 105
Anderson-Dixon, Nathan 94, **94**
Anjika (tiger) 78, **78**
Antonicic, James 98
Archaeology 69, **69**
Ashworth, Veronica 40
Auersperg, Alice 79
Avey, Anne Marie 104

B
Bailey, Bob 99
Baker-Stedham, Angie 16
Ballance, Gracie and Daisy 55
Baltic (dog) 11, **11**
Bandit (lizard) 87, **87**
Basketball, played by horse **5**
Bastable, Sharon Taylor 103, **103**
BEK (dog) 43, **43**
Bell, Matthew 17, **17**
Bennett, Tom **106–107**, 107
Bert (cat) 49, **49**
Bicycling, by parrot 32, **32**
Big Jake (horse) 86, **86**
Bindon, Sharon 31
Blanchard, Laurelee 14
Blind animals
  attacking robber 47
  guide cat for 33, **33**
  guide dog for 16, **16**
Blind people, guide animals for **6**, 36, **36**, 57, **57**
Bo (dog) **20–21**, 21
Bodeving, Karen 87
Bose, Rebecca 101
Bradley, Katie 22
Bragg, Richie 96
Bramble (owl) **30–31**, 31
Brody (dog) **106–107**, 107
Brook, Heather 53
Buczynski, Adam 11, **11**
Bundesen, Bryan 29
Burch, Mary 16, 96
Burke, Jane 28
Buttermilk (goat) 79, **79**

C
Cali (miniature horse) **6**, 36, **36**
Camels 94, **94**
Capybaras 15, **15**
Cardoza, Ed and Julie 32
Carr, Lisa 91
Casper (dog) 27, **27**
Cats
  attacking robber 47
  detecting low blood sugar 49, 89
  fashion for 62, **62**
  four-eared 98, **98**
  giant show cat 26, **26**
  gold teeth 37, **37**
  grumpy face 29, **29**
  guiding blind dog 33, **33**
  longest fur 104, **104**
  meeting owner at train station 105, **105**
  microchips 51
  prosthetic feet 95, **95**
  rescued by dog 45, **45**
  rescuing dogs 49
  rescuing people 46
  running for office 38, **38**, 61, **61**
  scootered by dog 64, **64**
  stealing things 97, **97**
  swimming **6**, 40, **40**
  traveling in suitcase 91
  with twenty-six toes 35, **35**
  two-colored face 92, **92**
  walking on ball 81, **81**
Cedric (horse) 24, **24**
Chamorro, Sergio 38
Charlotte (donkey) 91, **91**
Chase, Don 48
Cheesecake (capybara) 15, **15**
Chelsea (dog) 74, **74**
Chickens
  on leash 33, **33**
  mothering dogs 99, **99**
  rooster wearing boots 71, **71**
Chloe (dog) 57, **57**
Chris P. Bacon (pig) 56, **56**
Christensen, Alice 24, **24**
Cinders (pig) 34, **34**
Cobb, Karen 90
Cockatoos 79, **79**, 93, **93**
Colonel Meow (cat) 104, **104**
Combs, Adonna 13
Cooke, Melody 82
Cooper, Gwen 47
Cows
  fluffy 75, **75**
  jumping hurdles 100, **100**
  panda cow 55, **55**
Craig, Lori 25
Curley (donkey) 91, **91**
Curtis, Terry Marie 93

D
Dallas (cat) 51, **51**
Daniel (cat) 35, **35**
Danny (goat) 14, **14**
Darius (rabbit) 11, **11**
Davies, Rob 67, **67**
Diamond (dog) 29, **29**
Diamond (gerbil) 17, **17**
Dimock, Ingrid 33
Disabilities, animals with
  attacking robber 47
  cat with prosthetic feet 95, **95**
  guide cat for 33, **33**
  guide dog for 16, **16**
  pig with wheels for legs 56, **56**
Disabilities, people with
  guide dog for 57, **57**
  guide horse for **6**, 36, **36**
  helper monkey 98, **98**
Dogs
  as archaeologists 69, **69**
  attacking sheep 35
  buying video game points 50
  carried away by wind 89
  chasing burglars 87, 93, **93**
  detecting seizures 47
  dock diving 19, **19**
  doing tricks 15, **15**, 53, 85, **85**
  driving cars **4**, 58, **58–59**
  feeding sheep 54, **54**
  friendship with otter 74, **74**
  guarding wolf pups 101, **101**
  guide dog for blind dog 16, **16**
  guide dog for teenage runner 57, **57**
  hairstyles 25, **25**
  hang gliding **72–73**, 73
  jet skiing **106–107**, 107
  jumping rope 60, **60**
  mothered by capybara 15, **15**
  mothered by chicken 99, **99**
  mothering piglet 95, **95**
  mothering tiger cubs 78, **78**
  owl riding on 75, **75**
  painting pictures 41, **41**
  with pet owl **30–31**, 31
  playing soccer 43, **43**
  as Pup Scouts 71, **71**
  recycling 10, **10**
  rescuing humans 29, 46, **46**, 48, 96
  rescuing other animals 27, **27**, 45, **45**
  running road race 63, **63**
  scootering **7**, 64, **64**, 90, **90**
  stranded on ice 11, **11**
  swallowing pennies 37, **37**
  walking on "hands" 39, **39**
  walking with sheep 70, **70**
  wearing wigs **76**, 77, **77**
Donkeys
  helping horses 91, **91**
  rescuing sheep 35, **35**
  ridden by goat 14, **14**
  zedonks 41, **41**
Donor (dog) 74
Dotty (donkey) 35, **35**
Double-Dutch jump rope 60, **60**
Dozer (dog) 63, **63**
Ducks **6**, 66, **66**, 88, **88**
Dusty (cat) 97, **97**

E
Eddy (dog) 16, **16**
Elvis (cat) 62, **62**

F
Falcor (dog) 25, **25**
Farro, Steve 65
Fashion
  for cats 62, **62**

for ducks **6**, 88, **88**
for guinea pigs 23, **23**
Fay (duck) **88**
Fenne (giraffe) 13, **13**
Ferrets 69, **69**
Figaro (cockatoo) 79, **79**
Fitzpatrick, Noel 95
Flipper (rooster) 71, **71**
Florida (turtle) 51, **51**
Foster, Kyra 26, **26**

G
Garcia-Bengochea, Debbie 39
Geo (dog) 46, **46**
Gerbils 17, **17**
Geronimo (dog) 60, **60**
Gersbach, Jon 91
Gerstner, Sara 68
Gilbert, Jerry 86, **86**
Gilmore, Sandra 10
Ginny (dog) 58, **58–59**
Giraffes 13, **13**
Goats
    detecting seizures 61, **61**
    famous 79, **79**
    riding donkey 14, **14**
    skateboarding 82, **82**
    three-legged jumping goat 63, **63**
Godfrey-Brown, Judy 33
Godsell, Mark and Pam 63
Godwin, Susan 71
Goldie (chicken) 33, **33**
Goldie (dog) 45, **45**
Gorillas 12, **12**
Gracie Mae (cat) 91, **91**
Gradwohl, Michelle and Richard 55
Graeme (cat) 105, **105**
Grieser, Maria 43
"Grumpy Cat" 29, **29**
Guide cats 33, **33**
Guide dogs 16, **16**, 57, **57**
Guide horses **6**, 36, **36**
Guinea pigs 23, **23**, 67, **67**

H
Hamsters 55, **55**
Hamza, Jessica 105
Hang gliding, by dog **72–73**, 73
Hank (cat) 61, **61**
Happie (goat) 82, **82**
Harnish, Kathryn 79
Harper (dog) 15, **15**
Harrington, Brian 88
Harvey, Tom and Allie 78
Hercules (dog) 87, **87**
Higgins, Julie 46
Hilliard, Stewart 69
Hines, Pamela 69
Homer (cat) 47
Horses
    assisting blind owner **6**, 36, **36**
    flying in jets 24, **24**
    helped by donkeys 91
    indoors **102**, 103, **103**
    jumping 24
    painting pictures 13, **13**
    playing basketball **5**, 85, **85**
    tallest 86, **86**
    therapy horses 28, **28**, 39, **39**
Howard, Meagan 57
Huang, I-Wei 55
Huntington, John 33
Hyslop, Sheila 71

I
Inge, Lorna 93
Isabella (dog) 78, **78**

J
Jack (dog) 37, **37**
Jack (parrot) 65, **65**
Jackson, Gary 69
Jax (cat) 81, **81**
Jennifer (donkey) 91, **91**
Jenny (donkey) 14, **14**
Jess (dog) 54, **54**
Jesse (dog) **52–53**, 53
Jet skiing, by dog **106–107**, 107
Jets, horses flying in 24, **24**
Jett, Gretchen 47
Joe (camel) 94, **94**
Jordan (dog) **18**, 19, **19**
Jump rope 60, **60**
Jumping
    by dogs 19, **19**
    by gerbils 17, **17**
    by guinea pigs 67, **67**
    by rabbits 68, **68**
Jumpy (dog) 39, **39**
Jung, Amy and Ethan 89
Justin (horse) 13, **13**

K
Kai (dog) 101, **101**
Kasey (monkey) 98, **98**
Kate (kitten) 45, **45**
Katjinga (dog) 95, **95**
Keeble, Andrew 34
Kelleher, Tim 37
Kennedy, Ted 21
Kent, Mary Elizabeth 24
Knight, Erik 93
Knox, Randi Leigh 45
Krieger, Marilyn 97
Kuusk, Hannah 57

L
Latte (guinea pig) 23, **23**
Lautner, Matt 75
Lawhorn, Bruce 34
Lawless, Rob 79
Leopards 105, **105**
Levy, Kelly and Seth 91
Lili (dog) 49, **49**
Linden, Phoebe Greene 57
Lions 25, **25**
Lisa (rabbit) 105, **105**
Littler, Lee 87
Lizards 87, **87**
Lucero, Len 56
Lucien (horse) **102**, 103, **103**
Lukas, Mark 43
Luna (cow) 100, **100**
Luna (macaw) 83, **83**
Lynxie (cat) 64, **64**
Lyons, Leslie 92

M
Mabel (chicken) 99, **99**
Macari, Chloe 67
Macaws 32, **32**, 83, **83**
Mack, Lou 85, **85**
MacRae, Craig 13
Magarotto, Chiara 70
Magic (miniature horse) 39, **39**
Magidson, Susan 101
Manley, Sara 61
Martin, Samantha 81
Matilda (cat) 62
Max (cat) 62, **62**
Maximus (tortoise) 67, **67**
Mayer, Regina 100, **100**
McCarthy, Sean 19, **19**
McManus, Dan **72–73**, 73
Merlin (dog) 75, **75**
Mice **8–9**
Microchips 51
Migaloo (dog) 69, **69**
Miller, Pat 54
Milo (dog) 16, **16**
Miniature horses
    assisting blind owner **6**, 36, **36**
    playing basketball 85, **85**
    therapy horses 28, **28**, 39, **39**
Mitchell, Scott 12
Mizrahi, Shelly 85
Mog (cat) **6**, 40, **40**
Monkeys 98, **98**
Monty (cat) 49, **49**
Monty (dog) 58, **59**
Moorhouse, Louise 54
Morris (cat) 38, **38**
Mr. Binky (ferret) 69, **69**
Mudslinger (pig) 84, **84–85**
Music, played by pig 84, **84–85**

N
Nagelschneider, Mieshelle 89
Nakala (duck) 88
Nasira (tiger) 78, **78**
Nettle (dog) 99, **99**
Norman (dog) **7**, 90, **90**

O
Obama family 21, **21**
O'Duffy, Nichole 105
O'Leary, Matthew 61
Ootie (otter) 74, **74**
Orion (cat) 62, **62**
Oscar (cat) 95, **95**
Oscar (cockatoo) 93, **93**
Oscar (dog) 50, **50**

Otters 74, **74**
Owls 30–31, 31, 75, **75**

P
Paco (dog) 93, **93**
Page, Nan 74
Painting
    by dogs 41, **41**
    by horses 13, **13**
Panda (rabbit) 12, **12**
Panda cows 55, **55**
Panza, Rosana 63
Paquette, Gary 49
Parrots
    clucking like chicken 65, **65**
    pedaling bike 32, **32**
    rescuing children 57, **57**
    skiing 83, **83**
Paulchen (leopard) 105, **105**
Paulinchen (pig) 95, **95**
Payne, Christine 50
Peacock, Lorwi 75, **75**
Pendlebury, Elaine 35
Pennies, swallowed by dog 37, **37**
Pepper (rat) 27, **27**
Peter, Patricia 49
Petrina, Anthony 66
Pianezzi, Domingo 97, **97**
Pierce (sheep) 24, **24**
Pigs
    mothered by dog 95, **95**
    oldest 43, **43**
    playing music 84, **84–85**
    spa treatments 101
    surfing 2–3, 17, **17**
    wearing boots 34, **34**
    with wheels for legs 56, **56**
Pinky (dog) 96, **96**
Pippi (zedonk) 41, **41**
Pisco (alpaca) 97, **97**
Porter (dog) 58, **59**
Potsie (pig) 43, **43**
Preece-Kelly, Dale 42
Presidents, pets of 18, **20–21**, 21
Prince (goat) 61, **61**
Princess (hamster) 55, **55**
Pudding (cat) 89, **89**
Pwditat (cat) 33, **33**

R
Rabbits
    Flemish giant 11, **11**
    friendship with leopard 105, **105**
    jumping 68, **68**
    as pets for gorillas 12, **12**
Rae, Owen 100
Ramouni, Mona 6, 36, **36**
Ramsey, Rod and Michelle 46
Rats 27, **27**, 65, **65**
Recycling 10, **10**
Regina, Ruth 77
Riley, Charlie 46
Rochenski, Dianne 65
Rock, Ted 98
Roeser, Abby 27
Rogue (dog) 64, **64**
Roosters 71, **71**
Rosario, Eric 104
Rowdy (dog) 27, **27**
Rowell, Amy 35
Roz (tortoise) 22, **22**
Rupert (cat) 26, **26**

S
Samantha (gorilla) 12, **12**
Sammy (dog) 41, **41**
Sarah (duck) 88, **88**
Scooters
    dog scootering cat 64, **64**
    ridden by dog 7, 90, **90**
Sebastian (cat) 37, **37**
Service animals
    guide cat for blind dog 33, **33**
    guide dogs 16, **16**, 57, **57**
    guide horses 6, 36, **36**
    helper monkeys 98, **98**
Shadow (dog) **72–73**, 73
Sharp, Jackie 51
Sheep
    doing tricks 24, **24**
    fed by dog 54, **54**
    grazing on White House lawn 21
    rescued by donkey 35, **35**
    walking with dogs 70, **70**
Sid (dog) 85, **85**
Sidani (tiger) 78, **78**
Simon (dog) **76**, 77, **77**
Skateboarding
    by goats 82, **82**
    by mice 8–9
Skiing, by macaw 83, **83**
Skunks 42, **42**
Smith, Michele 45
Snoopy (rabbit) 68, **68**
Soccer, played by dogs 43, **43**
Sophi (dog) **30–31**, 31
Spero, Mitch 51
Stadelbacher, Mary 41
Stanley (sheep) 35, **35**
Steele, David 37
Steen family 29, **29**
Steiger, Mark 83
Stoner, Sami 57, **57**
Stoosh (skunk) 42, **42**
Strope, Greg 50
Stubbs (cat) 38
Sullivan, Ned 98, **98**
Surfing
    by alpacas 97, **97**
    by pigs 2–3, 17, **17**
Swimming, by cat 6, 40, **40**

T
Tardar Sauce (cat) 29, **29**
Tasha Bella (dog) 71, **71**
Tate, Edward 99
Tater Tot (miniature horse) 28, **28**
Teddy (dog) 48, **48**
Terfel (dog) 33, **33**
Texas Tornado (bull) 75, **75**
Therapy horses 28, **28**, 39, **39**
Therapy turtles 51
Tiger (cat) 46, **46**
Tigers 78, **78**
Tinkerbell (dog) 89, **89**
Tinkerbell (lamb) 70, **70**
Tortoises and turtles
    crocheted cozies for 22, **22**
    doing tricks 51, **51**
    long walks 67, **67**
Truffles (guinea pig) 67, **67**
Tubby (dog) 10
Tumbleweed (goat) 63, **63**
Turtles and tortoises
    crocheted cozies for 22, **22**
    doing tricks 51, **51**
    long walks 67, **67**

U
Utley, Lavern and Dorothy 89

V
Valle, Samantha 60
Venus (cat) 92, **92**
Vette, Mark 58
Vincent, John 84
Vinnie (rat) 65, **65**
Violet (horse) 91, **91**
Virginia (horse) 91, **91**
Von Muller, Omar 39

W
Wachter, Cherie 93
Wathen, C. W. 41
Wigs, for dogs **76**, 77, **77**
Williams, Jerry 65
Willie (parrot) 57, **57**
Willow (owl) 75, **75**
Wilma (pig) 101, **101**
Winiarski, Molly 15, **15**
Wise, Scarlett 70
Wolf, Janice 15
Wolves 101, **101**
Wright, Linda 64

Y
Yamada, Maki 23
Yoda (cat) 98, **98**

Z
Zachary (macaw) 32, **32**
Zalcman, Amy 37
Zebras 41
Zedonks 41, **41**
Zephyr (wolf) 101, **101**
Zoe (dog) 47, **47**
Zorro (pig) 2–3, 17, **17**
Zuerch, Michael 68

Credits

Cover: (UPRT), AP Photo/str; (Background), AP Photo/Kerstin Joensson; (LOLE), Kate Pinney

Back Cover: (UPRT), Abby Roeser; Mark Steiger; (LOLE), Kelley Miller/NGS Staff; (CTR), Amanda Edwards/WireImage/Getty Images; (RT), Omar Muller

1, Heather Brook; 2-3, Rambo Estrada; 4, SPCA/Caters News; 5, Kelley Miller/NGS Staff; 6 (UP), © South West News Service; 6 (CTR), AP Photo/Carlos Osorio; 6 (LO), Paul Lovelace/Rex USA; 7, Annette Redner; 8-9, Tim Marsden/Rex USA; 10 (BOTH), South Wales Argus; 11 (UPLE), Caters News/ZUMA Press/Newscom; 11 (UPRT), Annette Edwards; 11 (LORT), Institute of Meteorology and Water Management; 11 (LOLE), AP Photo/Maciej Czoska; 12, Associated Press; 13 (UP), Colin's Horseback Africa; 13 (LO), Adonna Combs; 14, Laurelee Blanchard/Leilani Farm Sanctuary; 15 (UP CTR), Brenda Winiarski; 15 (UPRT), DNY59/iStockphoto; 15 (LO), ZLD WENN Photos/Newscom; 16, Matthew Horwood/Caters News; 17 (UP), Donna Anastasi; 17 (LO), NZ Greenroom Productions; 18-19 (ALL), Steven Lankford; 21 (Background), Chip Somodevilla/Getty Images; 21 (INSET), Martin H. Simon/Pool via Bloomberg via Getty Images; 22 (BOTH), Katie Bradley/Caters News Agency; 23 (BOTH), Maki Yamada/Rex USA; 24 (UP BOTH), Alice Christensen; 24 (RT CTR), Sufi/Shutterstock; 24 (LO), Ashley Yanke; 25 (UP), Ren Netherland; 25 (LO), Jacqui Beluscak; 26, Chris Scott/Newspix Rex USA; 27 (UP), Abby Roeser; 27 (LO BOTH), Tribune Broadcasting/Getty Images; 28 (BOTH), Karine Aigner/National Geographic Creative; 29 (UP), Amanda Edwards/WireImage/Getty Images; 29 (LO), AP Photo/Damian Dovarganes; 30-31 (ALL) © South West News Service; 32, Karine Aigner/National Geographic Creative; 33 (UP), Tom Martin/Wales News Service; 33 (LO), Paul Miller/epa/Corbis; 34 (BOTH), © Ross Parry Agency; 35 (UP/CTR), AP Photo/Carrie Antlfinger; 35 (LO), PDSA; 36 (BOTH), AP Photo/Carlos Osorio; 37 (UP), Dr. David C. Steele; 37 (CTR), Tetra Images/Getty Images; 37 (LOLE), Ashley Lu; 37 (LORT), BluePearl Veterinary Partners; 38 (BOTH), Oscar Martinez/Reuters; 39 (UP), Omar Muller; 39 (LO), Kelley Miller/NGS Staff; 40 (UP), © South West News Service; 40 (CTR), Courtesy Veronica Ashworth; 40 (LO), © South West News Service; 41 (UP), Chestatee Wildlife Preserve; 41 (LO BOTH), Barcroft/Fame Pictures; 42, Dan James/Caters News Agency; 43 (UP), Becky Verdugo-Wong; 43 (CTR), Mary Martin; 43 (LO), Louis DeLuca/The Dallas Morning News; 45 (RT), Randi Knox/Anderson County PAWS; 45-49 (DOG AND CAT MEDALS), Janfilip/Shutterstock; 46 (UPRT), Carly Riley; 46 (CTR), Michelle and Rod Ramsey; 47 (UPRT), © Biosphoto/Superstock; 47 (CTR), James Jett; 48 (UP), Jean-Michel Labat/ardea; 49 (UP), Gary D. Paquette; 49 (RT CTR), Patricia Peter; 49 (LE CTR), Gary D. Paquette; 50, Karine Aigner/National Geographic Creative; 51 (UP), Dr. Mitch Spero; 51 (LO), Scott Manchester/Petaluma Argus-Courier; 52-53 (ALL), Heather Brook; 54 (BOTH), Richard Austin/Rex USA; 55 (UP), I-Wei Huang; 55 (LO), Happy Mountain Miniature Cattle Farm; 56 (ALL), Len Lucero, DVM; 57 (UP), Keith Stoner; 57 (LO), Tamara Reynolds Photography; 58-59 (ALL), SPCA/Caters News; 60, Steve Collier/Stunt Dog Experience TM; 61 (UP), AP Photo/Dang N. Le/Hank for Senate 2012 Campaign; 61 (LO), Sara Manley; 62 (ORIAN AND ELVIS), Leslie Masson; 62 (SAFRAM HALE BOPP AND MAX), AP Photo/Ed Ou; 63 (UP), Amanda Milczarski; 63 (LO CTR), Lydia C. Chandlee; 63 (LORT), Brooke Elizabeth Tyson of Brooke Tyson Photography; 64, Linda Wright; 65 (RAT), Eric Lorentzen-Newberg/Getty Images; 65 (PARTY HAT), Fotoksa/Shutterstock; 65 (CONFETTI), Ambient Ideas/Shutterstock; 65 (LO CTR), White Packert/Getty Images; 65 (LORT), Chester Zoo; 66 (ALL), The Peabody Memphis; 67 (UP), Duncan Simpson/Deadline News; 67 (LO), Matt Stewart/Caters News Agency; 68 (ALL), Marcus Scheidel/Startraks Photo; 69 (UP), Digital Photography By Joe & Suzy; 69 (CTR), Darren England/Newspix; 69 (LO), Mike Batterham/Newspix; 70 (ALL), South West News Service; 71 (UP/CTR), Susan Godwin; 71 (LO), Woodstock Farm Animal Sanctuary; 72-73 (ALL), Reuters/Jim Urquhart; 74 (ALL), Karine Aigner/National Geographic Creative; 75 (UPLE, CTR), Andrew Price/Rex USA; 75 (LO), Matt Lautner Cattle; 76, Brett Hufziger/Miami Beach; 77 (UPLE), Larry Aaronson/Chicago; 77 (UPRT/LOLE/LO CTR), Ruth Regina/Wiggles Dog Wigs; 77 (LORT), Modern Dog Magazine; 78 (ALL), Tom Harvey; 79 (UP), Took a Leap Farm; 79 (LO 1-3), Dr. Alice Auersperg; 81, Stacey M. Warnke; 82, Kelley Miller/NGS Staff; 83, Mark Steiger; 84, Dan Larson; 85 (UP), Steve Donahue; 85 (LO), Kelley Miller/NGS Staff; 86, AP Photo/Carrie Antlfinger; 87 (UP), From Nat Geo WILD's *Spoiled Rotten Pets*; 87 (LO), Rubert L. Littler III; 88 (LE/LO CTR), Paul Lovelace/Rex USA; 88 (LORT), Newspix/Rex USA; 89 (UP), Karine Aigner/National Geographic Creative; 89 (LO), K. Avenson Photography; 90, Annette Redner; 91 (UPRT), Rhonda Vanover; 91 (LO, BOTH), Karine Aigner/National Geographic Creative; 92, Courtesy VenusMommy; 93 (UPLE), LJSphotography/Alamy; 93 (UPRT), Exactostock/SuperStock; 93 (CTR) Sarah Reingewirtz/Pasadena Star News; 93 (LO), Cherie Wachter/Humane Society of Broward County; 94 (UP), Mikael Buck/Rex USA; 94 (LO), Frank Lukasseck/Getty Images; 95 (UPLE/UPRT), Roland Adam; 95 (LOLE/LORT), Jim Incledon; 96 (UP), Tylene Bragg; 96 (LO), Stephen Dalton/Nature Picture Library; 97 (UP), Pilar Olivares/Reuters; 97 (LO), Jean Chu DDS; 98 (UPLE), Pete Oxford/Minden Pictures; 98 (UPRT), Ivan de Petrovski; 98 (LO), BARM/Fame Pictures; 99 (UP), Adam Harnett/Caters News Agency; 99 (LO), Anita Maric/News Team International; 100, AP Photo/Kerstin Joensson; 101 (UP, BOTH), Rebecca Bose; 101 (LO CTR), From Nat Geo WILD's *Spoiled Rotten Pets*; 101 (LO RT), alejandrophotography/iStockphoto; 102-103 (ALL), Rex USA; 104, AP Photo/Guinness World Records/Ryan Schude; 105 (UP), Holger Hollemann/AFP/Getty Images; 105 (LO), Newspix/Trevor Pinder; 106-107, Fred Thornhill/Reuters

Credits

Copyright © 2014 National Geographic Society

All rights reserved. Reproduction of the whole or any part of the contents without written permission from the publisher is prohibited.

Published by the National Geographic Society
John M. Fahey, *Chairman of the Board and Chief Executive Officer*
Declan Moore, *Executive Vice President; President, Publishing and Travel*
Melina Gerosa Bellows, *Publisher; Chief Creative Officer, Books, Kids, and Family*

Prepared by the Book Division
Hector Sierra, *Senior Vice President and General Manager*
Nancy Laties Feresten, *Senior Vice President, Kids Publishing and Media*
Jennifer Emmett, *Vice President, Editorial Director, Kids Books*
Eva Absher-Schantz, *Design Director, Kids Publishing and Media*
Jay Sumner, *Director of Photography, Kids Publishing*
R. Gary Colbert, *Production Director*
Jennifer A. Thornton, *Director of Managing Editorial*

Staff for This Book
Robin Terry, Ariane Szu-Tu, *Project Managers*
JR Mortimer, *Project Editor*
Kathryn Robbins, *Art Director*
Simon Renwick, *Designer*
Kelley Miller, *Senior Photo Editor*
Rachel Korotkin, *Photography Intern*
Sharon Thompson, *Researcher*
Callie Broaddus, *Design Production Assistant*
Margaret Leist, *Photo Assistant*
Grace Hill, *Associate Managing Editor*
Michael O'Connor, *Production Editor*
Lewis R. Bassford, *Production Manager*
Susan Borke, *Legal and Business Affairs*
Madison Chapman and Paige Towler, *Editorial Interns*

Production Services
Phillip L. Schlosser, *Senior Vice President*
Chris Brown, *Vice President, NG Book Manufacturing*
George Bounelis, *Senior Production Manager*
Nicole Elliott, *Director of Production*
Rachel Faulise, *Manager*
Robert L. Barr, *Manager*

Based on the "Amazing Animals" department in *National Geographic Kids* magazine
Rachel Buchholz, *Executive Editor and Vice President*
Andrea Silen, *Associate Editor*
Kelley Miller, *Senior Photo Editor*
Stephanie Rudig, *Designer*
Nick Spagnoli, *Researcher*

Contributing Writers: Elizabeth Carney, Elizabeth Deffner, Richard De Rooij, Sarah Wassner Flynn, Kitson Jazynka, Jamie Kiffel-Alcheh, John Micklos, Jr., April Capochino Myers, Aline Alexander Newman, Tracy Przybysz, Kristin Baird Rattini, Heather E. Schwartz, Andrea Silen, C. M. Tomlin

The National Geographic Society is one of the world's largest nonprofit scientific and educational organizations. Founded in 1888 to "increase and diffuse geographic knowledge," the Society's mission is to inspire people to care about the planet. It reaches more than 400 million people worldwide each month through its official journal, *National Geographic*, and other magazines; National Geographic Channel; television documentaries; music; radio; films; books; DVDs; maps; exhibitions; live events; school publishing programs; interactive media; and merchandise. National Geographic has funded more than 10,000 scientific research, conservation and exploration projects and supports an education program promoting geographic literacy.

For more information, please visit nationalgeographic.com, call 1-800-NGS LINE (647-5463), or write to the following address:
National Geographic Society
1145 17th Street N.W.
Washington, D.C. 20036-4688 U.S.A.

Visit us online at nationalgeographic.com/books

For librarians and teachers: ngchildrensbooks.org

More for kids from National Geographic: kids.nationalgeographic.com

For information about special discounts for bulk purchases, please contact National Geographic Books Special Sales: ngspecsales@ngs.org

For rights or permissions inquiries, please contact National Geographic Books Subsidiary Rights: ngbookrights@ngs.org

Paperback ISBN: 978-1-4263-1459-9
Reinforced library binding ISBN: 978-1-4263-1460-5

Printed in Hong Kong
14/THK/1

A dog jumps through burning hoops during a pet competition in Hangzhou, China.